SEA STATE

SEA STATE

TABITHA LASLEY

4th ESTATE • London

4th Estate
An imprint of HarperCollins*Publishers*
1 London Bridge Street
London SE1 9GF

www.4thEstate.co.uk

HarperCollins*Publishers*
1st Floor, Watermarque Building, Ringsend Road
Dublin 4, Ireland

First published in Great Britain in 2021 by 4th Estate

1

A catalogue record for this book is
available from the British Library

ISBN 978-0-00-839093-8 (hardback)
ISBN 978-0-00-839094-5 (trade paperback)

Set in Dante MT Std
Printed and bound in Great Britain by
CPI Group (UK) Ltd, Croydon

MIX
Paper from
responsible sources
FSC™ C007454

FSC
www.fsc.org

For Mum, with love and gratitude

Every journalist who is not too stupid or full of himself to notice what is going on knows that what he does is morally indefensible.

JANET MALCOLM, *The Journalist and the Murderer*

Sigh no more, ladies, sigh no more,
Men were deceivers ever
One foot in sea and one on shore
To one thing constant never.

WILLIAM SHAKESPEARE, *Much Ado About Nothing*

This book is based on a series of interviews conducted over a six-month period. Names, workplaces and identifying features have been changed, to protect the privacy of interviewees. A few of the interviews are composites of several separate interactions; they have been condensed for the sake of narrative clarity, and also to anonymise the individuals featured. Any resemblance to actual persons, living or dead, is purely coincidental.

CONTENTS

There was one girl who came out to our rig. She was only nineteen. One night, she was playing pool in the rec room. She was wearing hot pants. Word got round, and the rec room started filling up. And up. And up. Soon, it seemed like every lad on the rig was in that room, sitting there, watching her play pool. She didn't get disciplined, she hadn't done anything wrong, but her supervisor did. They said: 'You should have told her, you should have let her know she can't do that here. That was your job, to tell her that, and you didn't do it.' As for the girl, she never came back. That was her first trip offshore. And her last.

ONE

T BLOCK

'Where's home?'

I was looking at his mouth as I said this. I'd never heard an accent like his before. It was a bit like mine (corrosive Scouse 'k'; some of the same distended vowels), but with a north-eastern melisma that turned *module* into *mod-joo-al*, *sure* into *shower*.

His lips were thin, yet gave the impression of fullness. They looked soft and malleable. His mouth was bracketed by two deep grooves that ran from either side of his nose to his chin and vanished when he smiled. I resisted the urge to insert a finger into one and push up, to see it disappear. As his lips parted and he prepared to speak, I saw the narrow gap between his teeth.

'Stockton,' he said.

★

On the road where my mother lives, there is a black spot where people sometimes die. They call it the bends. The area is semi-rural. Modern housing estates bisected by tracts of green. Markers of real countryside. Passing places, farm tracks, concealed entrances. The roads are wide, with a lazy camber that invites speeding. One night, we were driving down the bends, on the way back from Kinetic, and we crashed. It was November and it was raining. My boyfriend's car was a cheap little hatchback with slender tyres, and as he took a corner too quickly, the wheels lost contact with the surface of the road. The car slid across the tarmac like a blade over ice, tumbling through a metal gate, a fence, a hedgerow seamed with wire. I watched the hedge rushing up to meet us, illuminated in the headlights' glare, and thought that this time I would die.

We had crashed twice before, and I had a very clear sense, in those twirling, elastic seconds, that I was now out of chances. The boys in the back told me later that they thought I *had* died. They saw my head, in its blue Fila bucket hat, hit the roof three times and drop towards my sternum, the stem of my neck flopping ominously. But as the car came to rest in a ditch, and my boyfriend barked at his passengers to get out, get the fuck out, because beneath the bonnet the engine had started to smoke, I sat up and bit down. Between my molars, I could feel something like grit. Glass, smashed to a fine grain. I tried to open the door, but the barbed wire had wrapped itself around the car as we rolled, like twine around a spindle. I rattled at the handle, panic unfurling in my chest, and saw I was alone.

By the time I'd scrambled out of the door on the driver's side, my boyfriend was almost back at the bends. The car no longer looked like a car, but a pumpkin. The roof was crushed, the chassis splayed around the middle. There was no glass left in the windows or windshield. On impact, the steel had simply crumpled. I stared at it, too shocked to cry. How was it all five of us had walked away unharmed? Divine intervention. There could be no other explanation.

Except we weren't unharmed. The substance of the crash clung to me. For a long time afterwards, whenever I closed my eyes, I would see it: the veering headlights and bright spot of hedgerow, approaching far too fast. It still lurked beneath the waterline, and sometimes, when I was driving, I'd see it unfold in front of me. The car slipping out from under my control. Futile screech of brakes. Spiralling gravel, grass, birds, sky, soil. Black. Things ending with a crunch. Bone on concrete, slowly pooling blood.

Accidents happen when a few causal factors combine. An intersection of unlucky coordinates. Bad weather. Curving route. Young driver. Old car. The music didn't help: loud and propulsive enough to make him put his foot down. It was an old house tune (old even then, and this was twenty years ago) but its couplets had the cadence of a nursery rhyme, or a child's prayer.

When I go to bed at night, I think of you with all my might.
I love you. Fool.
Remember? Relate.

In some ways, he was the most instructive of all my boyfriends. He was two years older than me, at a time when that made a difference. He taught me things. His gospel relayed a frank and austere world I knew little of, but his lessons stayed with me forever. Some I passed on to other people. He taught me how to lace trainers so the knots couldn't be seen. How to tie a Berghaus in the middle so it still looked girly. He taught me – I still don't know how he knew about this – to put the soles of my feet together when I came, to intensify the pleasure. He taught me about hardcore before it became happy hardcore, how it used to have a breakbeat and a looming sense of doom.

He tried to teach me, with limited success, how to fight, how to throw a punch. He told me every boy must resign himself to being beaten at least once in his life. He administered several of these beatings himself, but he also received one, when a troop of unknown boys picked him up and carried him shoulder high through the train station, as a triumphant football team bears their captain around the pitch. Once inside, they dropped him onto the platform, stamped on his ribs and kicked him in the head. It was an unprovoked attack, an outpouring of tribal fury, and he accepted it without shame, without looking for reasons or seeking recompense. He knew the reasons. It was his cosmic bill come in. A tax on his maleness.

I love you. Fool.

He grew into one of those rare men who actually enjoyed physical confrontation. To him, chancing on the opportunity to brawl was like finding a tenner in the gutter. A minor stroke of luck which would nevertheless alter the course of his day, setting it on a cheerful, upwards trajectory.

One morning, about a month after the crash, I sent him to the shop for Rizla and Um Bongo. He returned twenty minutes later, looking pink in the face and exhilarated, as if he'd just been for a run. His white Ellesse tracksuit was soaked in blood. 'What have you been *doing?*' I said, as if I even needed to ask. The blood wasn't his, he explained, it belonged to someone else. At any one time he'd have several separate grudges going, and he'd spotted a boy he was feuding with, standing near the Rotary Club's yuletide float. My boyfriend took a bottle out of the bin, crept up behind him and hit him over the head with it. 'It was brilliant,' he said. '*Everyone* was watching. Father Christmas had ringside seats!' He ended up in Altcourse, where he flourished, like a green bay transplanted to its native soil.

Remember? Relate.

My term. My term was longer. I did remember, every day. I believed it was my own silent prayer (a wordless plea for benediction, uttered in a basal layer of my brain) that saved us. I refused to learn to drive for a long time. I hated getting in cars with anyone, even my mother, who drove everywhere at a ponderous twenty-eight miles an hour. That night, I found out fear is the strongest elixir. Whatever synthetics are coursing through your bloodstream, whatever chemicals have commandeered your limbic system, they will be neutralised. I was drugged when I got into that car, sober when I clambered out. And I've never forgotten that moment of gliding transition, the terrifying quickness with which conditions change. One minute, you have four wheels firmly on the tarmac. The next, you're turning cartwheels through the air.

*

I still thought of this place, its black spots and blind corners, its narrow roads and ruinous collisions, as home, though I hadn't lived there for years. I found myself picturing it before I went to sleep, its footpaths and fields, its closes of butter-bricked semis, and suburban ginnels of ficus and damp wood. These images came to me unprompted, like the old test card on television. I took comfort in them, their stasis, their bland, unchanging nature. I had lately lost my home. No. Not lost. That makes it sound unintentional, as if the bank had snatched it back after I'd defaulted on a mortgage payment. I had lately walked out on my home, and divested myself of the contents therein.

A few weeks after Christmas, a burglar broke into the flat I shared with my boyfriend and stole my laptop. He (I'm assuming it was a man, going by the footprint left on the panel of the door; like me, he was an Air Max One wearer) also took my old laptop, which I was using as a hard drive. I hadn't backed up anywhere else, so all my work went with it, including a book I'd been writing, off and on, for four years.

I let myself into the flat, failing to notice that the door was missing a panel. Adam abhorred waste, of any kind. It was quite unlike him to leave every light on, yet very like him to leave the flat looking – there really is no other way to put it – like it had been burgled. The drawers in my desk were upended, and the contents tipped out all over the floor. My first thought was that he'd been running late and had needed something from the desk. My second thought, barely formed before I realised what had actually happened, was that he'd gone rooting, looking for evidence of an affair. He was prone to occasional, highly specific fits of jealousy, and often went through my phone. I didn't keep a diary, but I had notebooks, and though it was understood he shouldn't read them, he did.

I walked into the bedroom, and saw then what had happened. The mattress had been turned, the sheets worried, my knickers lay in a tangled knot on the bed. A purse my sister had given me, with a sausage dog embroidered on the front, was emptied, turned inside out and discarded. She'd asked a few times if I liked the purse, because she'd never seen me use it. I went to the wardrobe, to check my most expensive shoes and my one good coat were still there. Air Max man though he was, the thief clearly didn't know decent clothes when he saw them. Or maybe he just couldn't envisage a use for them.

I looked around, and thought how meagre, how sad, our effects looked, strewn across the room. This was the sum of our life together, and it was all over the floor. The flat was one of those opportunistic London conversions, a home that would not exist outside the capital. It had once been a janitor's hut, tacked onto the back of a mansion block, and still had a menial look, beneath the modern fittings. I walked outside, for some reason still stopping to lock the door behind me, though half of it now lay in the kitchen, and called Adam.

'Go back in,' he snapped, when I finally got through to him. 'Go back in and get my weed.'

'I don't want to,' I said. I was standing on the drive outside our block of flats, shivering rapidly. The items in the flat, the flat itself, felt soiled, which at the time I attributed to this soft-footed presence, moving through the rooms unseen. Adam spoke slowly, as if talking to someone with a poor command of English.

'The police are coming, and I don't want them to find my weed. So will you go back in and get it, please?'

'They're coming to investigate a burglary,' I said. 'If they find it, they'll just assume it's his.'

The police closed the investigation after a couple of days. It was south-east London, they had more pressing matters to attend to than a purloined laptop. I kept hoping a memory stick might be slipped through the door, but that's what ethical thieves did, in places like Sweden. I went through my emails, and found twelve pages of my book. Other than that, it was gone.

For a week, I came back to the flat, shut myself in the bathroom and cried. In the evenings, Adam went out and patrolled the grounds, armed with his nine iron. Occasionally he would come into the bathroom, to wash his hands or brush his teeth, and step over me, a look of faint confusion on his face, as if trying to place this person who wept on his floor and ascertain why she was there.

At the end of January, I booked some time off work. I was going to go north: home for my mother's birthday, then on to Aberdeen for a week. I would start my book again. Only this

time, I would do it properly. My editor looked uncertain when I
told her my plans.

'It's cold in Aberdeen,' she said.

'It's also near the rigs.'

'What do you want to write about oil rigs for?'

'I want to see what men are like with no women around.'

'But *you'll* be around.'

I had friends at home who worked on the rigs. When we went
out together, they behaved as if they were famous, throwing their
money about and circulating busily, so everyone got a chance to
see them. Their reappearances were exciting, since they happened
only rarely, like a red moon or a partial eclipse. Most of the time,
they were away with work, or on expensive winter holidays.

Oil is one of the last avenues of blue-collar opportunity in this
country, one of the few sectors open to working-class men –
outside of sport – that still pays well. The oil workers I knew were
always trying to redress this imbalance by spending their wages
as soon as they got them. They bought powerful cars on finance,
expensive clothes, good shoes, strong cocaine. They went to the
gym, bench-pressed weights and covered themselves in tattoos (it
seemed a cultural practice somehow related to the job, as miners
in South Wales used to gather in chapel to sing). They stayed
single longer than most men in the provinces, and even their
marriages had a provisional feel, as if they might be dissolved at
any moment. They were *interesting*. The sort of people you'd
want at a house party, provided the house wasn't yours.

'The burglary was a sign,' I said. 'The book wasn't working. I
need to rip it up and start again.'

I was thinking here not of Adam, but of his best friend, who
nursed a brief obsession with new wave, and played that song
over and over again the summer we first met.

'It might not be a sign,' my editor said. 'It's January, your flat is easily accessible, and Adam decided to go round switching all the lights off before he went out.'

'I'm taking it as one.'

She put a hand on mine.

'I've often thought how hard it must be for you. Watching your little sister get married, when this relationship of yours is so on and off …'

'Marriage isn't important to me.'

'She's bought a house, you keep having to move.'

'She doesn't live in London.'

'Now she's having a baby …'

'Could we maybe stop talking about how everything is really good for my sister?'

I thought of my editor as motherly, though she couldn't have been much older than me. Perhaps it was because she was the same physical type as my mother: a pale-eyed, brittle brunette, easily moved to tears. She was a bit like the magazine editors of romantic comedies – the ones people said were implausible – in that she was heavily invested in my personal life and didn't care when my copy was late. She looked as though she was about to cry, probably because I was too. I really hated crying at work, though the casual observer might assume otherwise. She gave my hand a squeeze.

'One day, you'll meet a man who is so nice to you, you won't be able to believe it. It happened to me, when I met my husband. And I *know* it's going to happen to you.'

*

It takes two revelations to leave a person you've once loved. There is the moment you realise you no longer love them. And there is the moment you realise you can no longer pretend. The length of time between the two varies, depending on your capacity for deceit, your tolerance for fraud. Adam called me at my mother's house, the day before I left for Aberdeen. He'd received a cheque from the Inland Revenue, and was now four thousand pounds richer. I wondered if it was worth asking what he was going to do with the money, since I already knew the answer.

Unhappy couples always know how certain conversations will go. He was going to tell me that he planned to spend the money – all of it, every last penny – on himself. I was going to remind him that it was not two weeks since I'd lost the most precious thing in my possession. I'd say that for a writer, losing every word of your writing feels roughly equivalent to an early miscarriage. Then he'd snarl, 'I'm aware of that, I'm a writer too'. I'd reply, 'Not much of one' (it annoyed me that he always referred to himself as a writer, when he actually worked in PR, handling crisis management for an energy company). And he'd say something like 'You're fucking boring, do you know that?' For in the symphony of our discord, the gulf between his compromised ethics and my own, incorruptible art was a theme I liked to revisit.

It was probably true that I started more arguments than Adam, but he was better at finishing them. He'd sometimes hold his finger up to my lips, to let me know it was time to stop talking. If I tried to answer back, he'd say in a lilting voice: *Shhh. Shhh. Shut the fuck up now.*

'What are you going to do with that money?' I said.

'I'm going to buy a new iPad and pay off my credit card. I'll put the rest in savings.'

I shifted my position. I was sitting on the floor, and the ridges of the radiator were beginning to burn through the fabric of my T-shirt. We had been together five years. During that time, I'd left him twice. Ours was a fairytale romance: I had to fail twice before I could succeed. I had to learn to survive in reduced circumstances.

'Don't call me again,' I said. 'Just wipe my number from your phone. I'll do the same with yours.'

'What?'

I heard the breath of gas, then a click. He wasn't listening. I could hardly blame him. It wasn't the first time, or even the tenth, that I'd said this.

'Wipe my number from your phone. I don't want to hear from you again.'

'Is this about *money*?'

His tone sounded wounded, incredulous. Once again, his girl-friend was asking for something. Once again, her hand was out. She was like a Victorian urchin, a needful dependent. A maw.

'In part, yes. It's about the money. But it's about other things too. We're *miserable*, Adam. Aren't we? Please admit it.'

I checked myself, even as I said the words. It was this need for consensus that kept me trapped in his flat. I was determined to prove myself right, and he would never admit it. Even if the levy he paid was a wintry half-life with a woman he held in contempt.

'I was going to share it. If only you'd waited.'

For months, I'd lain awake next to him, as my nerves shrilled and my mind performed frantic, scuttling manoeuvres. Now, I felt calm. The realisation you're out of options brings with it its own brand of peace. I would leave him, I decided. I would leave him, his parents' money, and the shockproof captivity of moder-ate means. I would do it today. Then, whatever privations waited for me on the other side, I wouldn't have to do this again. I wouldn't have to hear him tell lies. I wouldn't have to watch him, wide-eyed as a hentai girl, swear, *swear*, that what he'd just said, he hadn't said, that what he'd just done, he hadn't done, that it was all just a figment of my febrile, female brain.

'No, Adam. You weren't. And that's fine. It's your money, you can do what you want with it. But I don't want you to call me again. So wipe my number.'

I sat for a while on the floor, looking out at the garden, the trees denuded of their leaves. Then I went upstairs and started to pack.

*

'What's that?'

'Nothing.'

I was looking at a list on my phone. I'd composed it on my way to Aberdeen: Adam's gravest infractions. I had thought, seeing as it combined two of my favourite pastimes – making lists, and meditating on his many faults – I might enjoy writing it, but it made for bleak reading. I ran out of stamina at the halfway point:

Family barbecue (his MOTHER!!!)
Making me walk up Scafell Pike in mist!!!
Mortgage fight
Dating site
Carla's wedding!!!
Soraya's hen!!!!!!!

'Do you want another drink?'

'I'll get these. What do you want?'

'No, you won't.'

'Why not?'

'You're a lass. Can't let you buy us a drink.'

He craned his neck to catch the attention of his friend, who was getting up to go to the bar.

'She'll have a Peroni.'

Peer-own-ee. There were six men around the table. They all spoke with the same singing modulations. Sweeter, more musical than accents from my corner of the country.

'Are we going to do this thing, then?'

'I suppose so.'

'I'll have to tape you, because my shorthand isn't all it should be. Also, I have to tell you I'm taping you. Otherwise it's illegal. Is that right? Maybe it's just not admissible in court, if you don't know you're being taped. Anyway.'

'What should I say?'

'Whatever you like.'

I put my phone on the table. He eyed it warily, as though it was an undetonated bomb.

'See, now I won't want to swear.'

'It's fine. You can swear. It's only my phone that will hear you.'

I watched him as he talked. He had a few pale freckles, scattered across the bridge of his nose. I had a weakness for freckles. I painted my own on with an eyebrow pencil: two stippled wings along the top of my cheekbones that usually merged into brown smears by the end of the day, making me look as if I went up chimneys for a living. He was complaining about a man he used to work with on the Brae Bravo. That he'd been given free rein to choose a topic, any topic, and had decided to talk about a colleague he hated made me like him more. I would have done the same.

'He was up on mod fourteen, fifteen, got the clamps, and started dropping them from the roof to the floor, just shutting them down! He was a nightmare. He was the worst Frenchman *in the world.* I didn't like him, he didn't like me. Said I was too cocky. Can't think why. He was in charge of us for a week. One day it was pissing down with rain, and he goes to me and this lad, "Youse are out there." I said, "I'm not going out there. It's *too wet.*" Just joking. Anyway, he went in and phoned the office, and ...'

On and on he ran, cataloguing the Frenchman's iniquities, which ranged from sticking a sign that said 'do not touch' on the thermostat in his room to taking a manway off a crane without a permit. The significance of most of these incidents escaped me, but I liked listening to his voice, its fractional echoes of home. Whenever I looked at him, he'd smile. There was a small delay as he looked back at me. And then he'd smile, with a quick, guilty motion, as though I was the foreman, and smiling at me was his job.

I had found him at the airport. He was standing near arrivals, listing under the weight of his kit bag. He was small, no taller than me. His body was compact and carefully proportioned, like a jockey's. He had a jockey's face too. Pliable and very pale.

'I'm looking for men like you,' I told him. 'I'm writing a book about offshore.'

'You going to slag it off?'

'What's your name?' I said.

He looked as though he might refuse to tell me. Then he said: 'Caden.'

'Well Caden, why don't you give me your number?'

'I wouldn't *dare* do that,' he said. 'I'm married.'

He got his friend Tyler to call me. Tyler told me to meet them at their hotel, where they were drinking with some other men. Offshore workers pass through Aberdeen with tidal regularity. Sometimes, they get stranded. In the summer, mist descends on the east coast and hangs there for a week, like grey gauze. In autumn, the weather takes a brutal turn. Super Pumas have a nasty habit of falling from the sky, and if the sea is too rough for rescue craft to sail, the choppers don't fly. The city is rich and dull. The winters are punitively cold. There is little to do but drink, and that's what stranded offshore workers do. They drink like it's their profession: starting as soon they get bumped, and committing to it for the next eight hours. They're driven partly by boredom (the dearth of daytime activities for squads of grown men), partly by the knowledge that once they're offshore, they won't be able to drink at all.

The men looked up as I walked into the bar, mild expectation on their faces. Caden was sitting in the corner, staring at a list of runners on his phone.

'Help me pick,' he said, barely glancing up. I didn't gamble enough to be guided by anything other than the name. 'That one,' I said, pointing to Anonymous John. 'Go for that one there.'

They were on their way to the T Block, but were unwilling – or unable – to supply more details than that. It was possible they didn't know where they were in relation to other rigs. Maps don't tell you much, since oil companies, like pay per view channels, only acknowledge their own assets. Everyone was talking about the price of Brent Crude, and the tumble it had taken. Oil is a volatile commodity, its price linked to geopolitics and economic growth, as well as supply (which is inelastic) and demand (which tends to be cyclical). Ever since the first North Sea crude oil came onshore, in the seventies, it's been locked in a boom–bust cycle, though this downturn appeared more serious than the last. Put simply, the market was saturated. The machines designed to do our bidding had spun out of control, like the sorcerer's enchanted broom. They kept churning out cheap product – Iran Heavy, Arab Light, Dubai Crude, Qatar Marine even as the price was falling fast.

On the way to the hotel, my taxi driver had spoken at length about Aberdeen's profligacy, its reckless reliance on one revenue stream. People put their eggs in one basket, and lived beyond their means. You saw them driving around, in their Range Rovers on finance, with their big houses on Morningfield Road. As if they could afford it! It was a myth that oil workers earned huge salaries, a piece of propaganda left over from the eighties, mostly put about by the workers themselves, but only when it suited them. The money used to be good, but the industry had been neglected. They were out of sight and out of mind. Of course they'd had recessions before – they were down to nine dollars a barrel in 1999 – but this was different. This was the industry preparing for the future. There was a sermonising tone to his talk; he sounded quite pleased. He used to work offshore, but got out when the going was still good. Like every taxi driver in Aberdeen, he had once worked offshore.

I pushed my phone towards the man sitting opposite me.

He unloaded various grievances: the cost of the mail flight back to Teesside; the way oil companies expected contractors to drop everything and travel three hundred miles with a few hours' notice; the class divide offshore. He was the oldest man at the table, and the best looking, by some margin. His eyes were black, his cheekbones high and slanted. He appeared to be mixed race, though it took me a while to register this. What's obvious and unremarkable in London becomes shifting and indeterminate somewhere like Aberdeen.

'There's over a thousand men out of work now. Lads are applying for jobs and getting their CVs sent back, or replies saying "Sorry, but there's six hundred looking at the same job".'

'When will the price go back up?'

'They reckon it'll get better by next month. End of March, everything will be back to normal.'

Tyler's voice sailed over the collective burr. He was complaining about women. A man from the Tern had gone on *Take Me Out*. Before he'd even stepped onto the stage, every girl had switched her light off. I thought how nice it was, being around men who watched *Take Me Out*. Adam didn't like me watching ITV. He called it the 'northern channel'.

The afternoon wore on, the sky grew dark. We swapped stories. I offered a brief précis of the past month. The men shook their heads and commiserated.

'What was your book about?' said the one sitting to my right. He had a long, lugubrious face under a wedge of grey hair.

'This, really,' I said, looking at Tyler. 'What it does to your relationship, having someone gone half the time. How the women at home cope.'

'It's hard,' he said. 'You shouldn't plan things for your first week back. You always end up missing them. There was a lad who got stuck on the Central, missed his own wedding.'

'That sounds like a punchline to a joke.'

'Don't think his lass found it funny.'

The grey-haired man was getting married that summer. He showed me a picture: a delicate blonde, younger than him, dandling a baby on her knee. It was passed around the table to generalised congratulation. Next to me, Caden murmured something.

'What did you say?'

'Weddings. They're a nightmare.'

'I think weddings are fun.'

It was one of those lies that was, even at the time of telling, inexplicable. I did not think weddings fun at all. An invite to late spring nuptials, in some far-flung rural outpost, could throw me into the sort of temper more often associated with being left off the guest list altogether.

'Getting married is pointless. It's a waste of money.'

I was surprised that the thought of wasting money might pain him. His wallet was thick with notes, and every time he got up to buy more drinks, crumpled twenties fell out and floated down towards the floor.

'Not if you're a woman. It makes economic sense. You don't have any claim on your boyfriend's assets if you break up, even if you've got children. People always think they do, but they don't.'

'I'll tell you this, right. No man ever wants to get married. It's always for they girlfriends.'

I tugged at my necklace. It was a nervous habit; dragging the crucifix back and forth, testing the chain's tensile strength. The necklace was fine, and I knew that if I continued to pull it, one day it would snap. And yet I couldn't stop.

'Didn't you want to get married to your wife?' I said.

Around us, the noise ebbed and swelled. His gaze drifted over to the bar and back. His phone flickered to life and he picked it up.

'Third on that. Each way we done. We've got back twenty quid.'

Snow was starting to fall. My phone lay on the table, forgotten, recording the crosscurrents of conversation. It would take hours to transcribe. Six different voices, their accents indistinguishably similar, all talking over each other.

'His lass tracked him to a strip club last night.'

Caden's lips were close to the whorl of my ear. We were both watching Tyler. He had a handsome, darkly flushed face. More teeth than the average person. He looked like a man who was successful with women, and would pay for it anyway. He was telling a story about his last trip home. He'd been dropped off in Edinburgh too late to find a room, and had struck some sort of deal with a homeless man. The content of the story was boring, but his delivery was pacy and dramatic. People were actually putting their drinks down to listen.

'You shouldn't go to strip clubs.' I said. 'It's demeaning. As long as there are strip clubs, there will be men who think women's bodies are for sale.'

'I never buy dances,' said Caden. 'I don't see the point. I just go there for a drink. I've never paid for anything, me.'

'No.' My eyes settled on his face. 'I don't suppose you'd have to.'

He glanced down at the table. Colour was building in his cheeks. His freckles glowed, backlit by the blush.

'Tyler's lass put that Find My iPhone thing on his phone. Soon as he walked in, she text him saying "I know where you are".'

'Really?'

'True story.'

'That's … *insane*.'

'That's what it's like at home.'

'Where's home?'

I was looking at his mouth as I said this. His lips were pink against his pallor. His eyes were blue and very clear, as if he'd never entertained a sin.

'Stockton,' he said.

He told me some things about his hometown. A place where husbands had to be captured and corralled like Camargue horses, and struggled in their bridles even after marriage. Where all the men worked offshore, and nights were enlivened by scheduled violence and bouts of wifely thuggery. Towns were quicker to progress the closer they were to a city's civilising sphere. Stockton-on-Tees was near nothing: an empty, unsupervised hinterland.

'I've got a theory about women on your side of the country,' I said. 'They're rough. I remember going to see my friend in Nottingham. There were women fighting with their fellas on the street. And *winning*.'

This theory was based on nothing much, apart from a few scraps of anecdotal evidence, but he nodded as if it were established fact.

'My cousin's pretty hard. She goes out and fights. When she has to. She's the only woman I'm physically scared of. Slammed us into a door when I was fifteen. I've still got the scar.'

'Where?'

'Just there.'

There was a jagged indentation at his hairline. I reached up and traced it with my fingers. He jumped, as at a small electric shock. His hair stood away from his forehead in an airborne crest. I ran a hand over it, smoothing it down against his brow. There was a slight curl to it, a hint of resistance in its texture. I continued smoothing long after it lay flat, transfixed by the motion, the proximity of his skin. He sat there, letting me do it. A pulse fluttered at his temple. I touched it, and it quickened.

'You have messy hair,' I said eventually. 'You should invest in a comb.'

*

'You're a whore.'

'What did you say?'

'You're a whore. You're easy.'

I looked at the man who had spoken. He was tall, with a big, square skull. Columns of ink crept above his collar.

'I can't be both,' I said. 'A whore is, by definition, not easy. You have to pay. So am I a whore, or am I easy? Which one is it?'

The big man was vacillating, a pained look on his face. He looked upset at being forced to choose.

'You're easy,' he said, after a moment.

'You're rude.'

Caden put a hand on my arm. His touch was so warm. His inner thermostat must have run a little higher than mine.

'Calm down,' he said, under his breath.

He was stroking my hand, as you might stroke a large Molosser dog about to maul a houseguest. And there was something canine about the way I quivered under his touch. I was always like this when I drank: torn between the instinct to fight and to fuck, my superego trying to mediate between two contrary directives.

I addressed the man. 'How dare you? Say you're sorry.'

The man sat in profile to me. He stared out in front of him, like a face hewn into a cliff. Stern, meditative, untroubled by the turn the conversation had taken. Why should he be? It was he who had steered it onto the rocks.

'I'll buy you a drink if you want. I'm not saying sorry.'

'I can buy my own drinks. I don't want a drink. I want an apology.'

'You'll not get one,' he said with dignity. 'You're easy. There. I said it. Because I saw it.'

Caden's fingers were under my cuff. He ran them over the inside of my wrist. It was a strangely intimate gesture, though he barely grazed the skin.

'You need to leave it,' he said. 'But you can't, can you? I can see that.'

'No. I can't.'

The man was drunk. It was possible he hated all women. Still, I felt implicated by what he'd said. He was staring into the middle distance, with the lucid calm of a clairvoyant. There was a no-hard-feelings tenor to his attack. Maybe he had seen it. Maybe he knew something about me I didn't know myself. I tugged my hand from Caden's grip, spilling his drink as I did, and jumped up, so the stool behind me tipped, swayed, then fell. I stepped back, surveying the minor pocket of chaos I'd created. Caden dabbed at the pooling liquid with his sleeve.

'You'll have to toughen up if you want to write about offshore,' he said. 'The rules are different out there. This is how lads talk.'

I left then, making my way up the spiral staircase and out into the night. He stood up and followed me, just as I knew he would.

We stood outside, our teeth clattering companionably. There was ice on the ground. I was dishevelled, in layered wool and a thick parka (bought that morning, after I walked out of the hotel and realised the coat that had seen me through a London winter really wouldn't do). He was wearing a little waterproof jacket that gave him the look of a football casual but offered no protection against the cold. There were snowflakes in his hair.

'Where are you going?' he said.

'I don't know.' I shifted from foot to foot. The bar was in the basement, and the lower half of our legs would still be visible from the window.

'It's still early.'

'It feels late. I might just go back to the hotel and sleep.'

It could have been any time between five and nine. I was disorientated by the rapid onset of the dark, the early drinking.

'That lad. I know it doesn't make it right, but he's from the roughest bit of Stockton. I'm not sure if he …'

He looked about him, as if he might find more mitigating information on the floor. His face was level with mine. He looked simultaneously older and younger than me: boyish bone structure, worn skin. Baby-faced, he might have been called, in a different era. Although he wasn't. Not quite.

'Thank you for letting me come out,' I said. 'Sorry it went a bit wrong.'

'I feel weird about you going. I've known you longer than I've known him.'

It was the sort of distinction a child might make. Or someone with a child's skewed sense of time. By now, we'd walked a little way up the road, and stopped by some wrought-iron railings. There were still a few avenues left open to us, though the pretence he'd left the bar only to see if I was all right after the nasty man had called me a bad word was becoming less believable with every step we took. The snow was falling more heavily now. It spun around us where we stood, in wind-whipped eddies and spirals. The streets were deserted, the city driven in by the cold. Under the camouflaging dark, it was easy to believe we were invisible, and could remain so as long as we liked.

'I have to go now,' I said.

The truth, as he must have known, was that I had nowhere to be. It's dangerous, to strip people of their routines then tell them to fill their time wisely. Above the funnel of his collar, his face was white and vulnerable. He looked frozen. I went to kiss his cheek, and as I leant in to close the final gap between us, he turned his head, so that his mouth was on mine. Even as he did it, I was aware the night could still be rectified. I could purse my lips and transform the kiss into something sealed and comparatively chaste. Not a kiss you'd give your mother, but one you might plant on a friend. There would be space between what had happened and what we would pretend, but it would be slippage. A small, survivable loss. But I didn't want to. I didn't want to. What I wanted was for us to be alone. What I wanted was all of his attention, trained on me. His hands on me. His mouth on me. I could smell his skin. I'd forgotten what this was like. Comprehensive need. To be so soaked in another person's presence that everything else cedes, as to floodwater. I stood there for a moment, flooded. Then I reached around, pulled his head down, and kissed him back.

He pulled away first. He was slightly out of breath.

'Come here,' he said.

He took hold of my crucifix. It had migrated sideways, and now lay below my clavicle. For a moment, I thought he was going to snap it off, but he simply ran it back along its chain.

'Sorry. Been wanting to do that all afternoon.'

Our breath smoked before us. My hands were mottled with the cold: white, purple, red. I took my gloves out of my pocket, pulled them on and watched as he did the same. I'd never been in a city where all the men wore gloves before.

'Come with me,' I said. 'If you want.'

I held a hand out towards him. He took it in his. I thought he might hesitate, make a show of being torn, and was curiously impressed when he didn't bother. We set off, walking through the silent, windblown streets, and neither one of us looked back.

*

That night, I found out several things. That his mouth was as malleable as it looked. That his kisses were weightless things. That his wife did not trust him an inch, for his phone rang constantly, and though he walked out of earshot every time he picked it up, I could tell from the frequency of her calls, and the staccato pattern of their contact, that they were fighting. I didn't understand provincial marriages, I thought, as he got up for the fourth time and walked off with the phone pressed to his ear. I'd lived away too long.

We stopped at a bar on Belmont Street. There had been some effort to dress it up in Scandinavian style: pale wood, bench seating, a freezer full of flavoured vodka. On a screen above the terrace, Aaliyah cooed to a falcon on her wrist. I'd spent more time than I should have seething over the hipster appropriation of Aaliyah ('I liked her before she was dead!' I wanted to yell, like Piggy, with the conch). To learn that the culture of your youth has been absorbed and spat out by the twenty-year cycle is to be reminded you're really too old to be out.

He came back in. His jacket was damp, his hair stuck up in a single, snow-slicked tuft. I smoothed it back down.

'You look about twelve,' I said.

He grinned. There was a beady complacency about his smile I hadn't noticed before. He leant in towards me. His breath was sweet.

'I am about twelve. The police will be here soon.'

I wrapped my legs around him, and pressed my nose against the base of his neck. The bar was quiet, though perhaps not quiet enough to excuse such poor behaviour. I couldn't remember the last time I'd been kissed with comparative hunger. I couldn't remember the last time I'd been kissed. Adam and I had never stopped fucking, never achieved that companionable merger when a couple grows so close they become siblings, but this spiky electricity came at a cost. I knew now why prostitutes refused to kiss their johns.

I caught a hank of his hair in my hand, and tipped his head back. His skin was soft, its grain finely sifted. Edible, I thought, putting my mouth to his throat. He wriggled out from underneath me. There was a perfectly executed oval of tooth marks on his neck. His hand flew to it.

'Is that what I think it is?'

'Depends what you think it is.'

He got up to buy more drinks. As he queued at the bar, his phone began vibrating. I watched her name flash urgently: *Rachel*. Wives should always have trochaic names. Mistresses were like strippers; they had to be iambic: Natasha, Sofia, Saskia. Assia. What would happen if I picked up and told her where he was? I could picture it – a kind of interpersonal *appel du vide* – the way I could sometimes see myself falling under the tube on the way home from work, breaching the yellow line and slipping down onto the tracks.

When he sat back down, he smiled at me. He had what I thought of as a lateral smile. It extended out, rather than up, beyond the curve of his palate.

'You've got … dead big eyes, like.'

'You sound like Little Red Riding Hood.'

He tried again.

'You've got … dead nice teeth.'

One of my incisors was twisted. Reflexively, I ran my tongue over it. At school, I'd worn braces. They never quite corrected the errant tooth, but they'd been useful in other ways. I'd learnt the lesson every snaggle-toothed teen ingests. Deploy your smile sparingly, and people will fight harder to see it.

'You still sound like Little Red Riding Hood.'

I pulled my lip up into a snarl, snapped my teeth at him, and lunged. He caught hold of my wrists, giggling. Then his grip tightened and his expression changed.

'Like it rough, do you?'

'Sometimes.'

'Let me come back with you. I can't grab you the way I want out here.'

'I think that's a bad idea.'

'Why?'

'You're married, you're miles from home, you're off the chain. Don't waste this opportunity on a woman who won't fuck you.'

'Why won't you fuck me?'

Because my legs and armpits wore their winter pelt of hair. My bikini line had not been attended to since Christmas. My toenails were unvarnished, and jagged as claws; my underwear fit only for the first day of a period. Also, I suspected I smelt. I'd showered that morning, but it was late, and I was wearing leather leggings. The leggings were in need of a wash, but cleaning them was a specialist job, one that would mean parting with them for three weeks. That morning I'd looked at them, thought of the nest of bacteria doubtless swarming in the crotch, and told myself I would not, could not, wear them again. Then I'd looked outside, considered the cold, the limited options in my suitcase, and, uttering a silent promise to my vagina that this would be the very, *very* last time it happened, put them on again.

'I'm not at my fighting weight,' I said. 'I'm at my walking around weight.'

'So what?'

'So I can't take my clothes off in front of a stranger.'

He gave me a smile that told me the matter was settled.

'But we're not strangers any more. Are we?'

*

'Luke was gutted his lass wasn't pretty.'

We sat on the bed in my hotel room, drinking beer. Luke had been drinking with us earlier. He was the youngest of the men, the only one from Aberdeen. His girlfriend came to meet him and instead of bringing her down to the bar, he kept her outside, smoking. We passed them as we left.

'I don't think that's true,' I said. 'I think it's more likely that he wanted to spare her your colleagues, and their charming, progressive views.'

'He was *gutted*. Listen, if his lass was nice, he would have brought her down. She wasn't. So he didn't.'

'She wasn't not pretty. She just wore glasses.'

Was she pretty, or was she just young? With every year that passed, I found it harder and harder to distinguish between the two states. Either way, I was disappointed in him. For some reason, I'd assumed that men who worked at such extremes might be above this sort of talk, that they'd rate their wives and girlfriends along a worthier index (strength? Agency? Capacity to bear children, who could then be sent to work down the pit?).

'Can I ask you something?' he said.

I took a sip of my beer, and lay down next to him. He had taken off most of his clothes. The clean-sheet smell of his neck was rising off him in concentrated draughts. Clothed, he looked a bit wan, a bit undernourished. Undressed, his body was a marvel of scaled-down perfection. His muscles were curved and hard. The skin below his ribs was softer than mine. I ran my hand over his chest, wondering at the frantic self-love, the dose of conceit, it must take to maintain this condition past the age of twenty-four.

'You may.'

'What did you think of me when you first saw me?'

'You're like a bird. I *always* used to ask men that.'

'Tell me.'

'I thought that you were small. And then I saw that you had *Wood Group* written on your bag, and thought you probably worked offshore.'

'Is that it?'

'Yes,' I said, dropping a kiss on his temple. 'That's it.'

He frowned. He was dissatisfied with this answer. As I would have been, had our situations been reversed.

'Don't you want to know what I thought of you?'

'Not really.'

'Why not?'

'Because I don't care.'

'I thought you fancied Tyler.'

'Did you now?'

'I thought you were flirting with him.'

'That's not how I flirt.'

I sat on top of him, my thighs on either side of his chest. His mouth looked bruised, succulent. I kissed it, and then the indigo stain I'd left on his skin. I was sorry now that I'd put a mark there, not because it would embarrass him, but because I'd spoiled the white perfection of his throat.

'So did you?'

I paused. My lips were pressed against his neck.

'Did I what?'

'Fancy Tyler?'

I sat up.

'If I fancied Tyler, I'd be here with Tyler.'

He lifted his head a few degrees from the pillow.

'Why are you still dressed? Christ, you've still got your fucking Air Max on!'

My clothes came off, in grudging increments. He was restricted in what he could do, since I refused to remove my underwear. I was reminded of evenings in my teenage bedroom: boys' hands making little sallies under my school skirt, my temperate consent, issued by way of a slackening, an absence of fight.

He squirmed beside me. His body was hot and anxious. I could feel his erection against my thigh. He got harder than other men. I knew this was a quirk of chemistry, and felt more fiercely wanted, all the same.

'You know what you are?' he said. 'A cock tease.'

'Do people still say that?'

This too was a sentiment I'd last heard expressed at school.

'Aye. If someone's cock teasing them.'

'Cock teasing isn't a thing. What you mean is women not capitulating to what you want straight away.'

My fingers made contact with the silky panels of skin below his ribcage. I turned around, so I could press myself against him and inhale the scent of his neck. I took his hand, guided it under the elastic of my knickers (ugly, threadbare, high-waisted things) and between the lips of my cunt. I allowed it to remain there for a second before twisting away, so he could see what he had done.

'You're not going in there,' I said, in what I judged to be a reasonably accurate approximation of his accent. 'It's *too wet!*'

I'd not undressed in front of anyone, other than Adam, for more than five years. This person was different in every way (smaller and slighter, but stronger; more dogged and persistent in his pursuit of sex, but more attentive, and almost painfully keen to please), but he was the one who seemed familiar. Sitting opposite him, watching him talk, seeing his little face crease as he laughed, I felt a rush of proprietary recognition, as if I'd spotted a book I once loved and lent out languishing on someone else's shelf: hold on, that's *mine*. Why is it here?

He put his hand over my mouth. I could taste the metal of his wedding ring, melded with my wetness on his fingers.

'You know I can't see you again after this, don't you?' he said.

I tried to nod. Beneath his palm, I was pinioned in place.

'If we don't have sex now, we won't be able to, ever. Are you okay with that?'

I made a muted sound behind his palm. He loosened his hold.

'I'm okay with that.'

'You sure?'

He pulled my bra down and pushed my breast up, into his mouth. I stroked his hair, my hand working its way round to the back of his head. He took this as his cue to suck harder. I winced as my nipples hardened under his tongue and his teeth snagged at the skin. There would be a bruise there in the morning.

'Yes,' I said. 'I'm shower.'

I once shared a room with a rigger who was on Piper Alpha. What he told me was this: he was up on the helideck, the heat was burning his hair, but he was feart to jump. There was an older guy, trying to will him on and he wouldn't do it. So the old guy ended up grabbing hold of him and jumping. When they hit the water, the old guy's life jacket came up, broke his neck and he died. The lad told me this after we'd been sharing a room for about a week. He still seemed very affected by it. He didn't speak much, he didn't socialise, he didn't really leave the room. He just stayed in there, reading.

TWO

FOUM ASSAKA

'He's not going to turn into John Updike. You know that, don't
you?'

I had bought Caden a copy of *Villages*. Tom tapped the book's
spine.

'Even if he reads it. He still won't know the difference between
too and *to*.'

Tom was my sub-editor. We were visiting his auntie, who lived
in a village outside Aberdeen. Her son worked on a drill ship
moored off the coast of Morocco, and she thought it might be
useful for the two of us to meet.

'Good writers are usually good readers,' I said, putting the
book back in my bag.

Their house was strangely configured. The bedrooms were in
a sunken row below ground, while the kitchen was on the first
floor, overlooking the larches. It was like sitting in a tree house. I

hoped Tom would drop the subject before his cousin came back upstairs, but could think of no way of saying this that didn't make me sound unduly concerned with his opinion.

Tom pecked at his phone.

'Listen to this: *The first breath of adultery is the freest. After that, constraints aping marriage develop.*'

I tapped him on the shoulder.

'Wrong book.'

The truth was, I did feel constrained, by knots of my own binding. I was never sure how much of Caden's pull was manufactured by his tantalising patterns of absence and delay. I just knew his fleeting appearances in my life (like a celebrity doing a club PA, he ducked in, then out, leaving me with a large bill and the uneasy feeling I'd been ripped off) were not enough.

The last time I saw him, his chopper was late to the rig, so he missed his flight to London. He bought me a flight to Aberdeen instead, and I left Heathrow at eight. 'Won't your wife notice?' I said, thinking of the inexplicable dip in their bank balance. 'No, no,' he soothed. 'It's the business account. She doesn't know anything about it.'

As my plane approached Aberdeen, it was diverted to Edinburgh because of fog. It sat on the tarmac for an hour. They played the collected hits of Donna Summer over the tannoy – '(If It) Hurts Just A Little'; 'This Time I Know It's For Real' – and told us nothing. Then we were herded into taxis and driven up the spine of the country. I didn't reach him until two in the morning. By the time we got to the hotel, I was too exhausted to speak. He took my dress off, and I sat in my underwear, my legs folded around his waist, as he talked to Virgin, and explained why I wouldn't be on the first flight back.

'It's for my girlfriend,' he kept saying to the person at the other end. 'I need to change the ticket for my girlfriend.'

The next morning, he flew home at seven. Between us, we spent nine hundred pounds, and bought five hours in each other's company. 'You're like a very expensive prostitute,' I said as I watched him dress, though the comparison was generous. I couldn't, in good conscience, class what we'd done as fucking, any more than I'd call a speculum a sex toy. Had I paid for it, I'd be asking for a refund. Yet when he left, I felt as I did before. Like someone had reached down my throat and ripped out something vital. I texted him as he waited to board: *My heart hurts*. And so it did, an inward ache for which I had no salve. *Mine does too*, he replied. *It wants to be with you*. I told him he shouldn't say that, even if he meant it. I suffered these occasional twinges of bad conscience. In the space of a day, my sympathies aligned with him, realigned with her, then drifted back to him again, as the sun drifts in and out from behind a cloud.

'You know the thing about these stories?' Tom said. 'They always end the same way.'

'What always ends the same way?'

Tom's cousin Callum had reappeared, with a bottle of wine.

'Your Nana's stories. Tom said they tend to be quite gothic.'

Callum pulled an adjudicating face. His features were quite different to Tom's, but the spatial relation between them was similar, so at first glance they looked alike. And every so often, I'd look up and see him make one of Tom's expressions, as he was doing now.

'I've never heard that one about Miss Hamilton before.'

Last night, their grandmother had talked about her time as a nurse. Miss Hamilton was a patient. The woman was a simpleton, she said, committed for life. She was born blind and completely bald, with a scalloped ridge of flesh running the length of her scalp, like a cockscomb. She had perfect pitch, and a voice like a glass bell. She used to sing arias in the day room, her high, clear soprano lifting the hairs on the necks of the orderlies and making the piano strings shiver in sympathetic resonance.

'I feel like you would have remembered it, if you had.'

Tom's cousin put a dish of lasagne on the table and motioned for us to eat. He reached over to fill my glass.

'What was your book about?' he asked.

'It was about a diver. His wife finds out he's having an affair, and moves the family out to a marsh.'

'I thought about diving for a bit. Until I met a few divers. They've all got that thousand-yard stare.'

Pioneer divers were sacrificed on the new frontier. Crippled by fifty, dead by sixty. A litany of health complaints that chased them to the grave. They sent them too deep in the eighties. It's not safe to go below one hundred and eighty metres. They didn't know that then.

'Someone told me they never sue, because most come from the navy,' I said.

'No compensation culture,' said Callum.

'I was at school with a girl whose dad did it,' I said. 'He killed himself in the end. Her family said he got the bends one too many times. It drove him mad. It was her I was thinking of when I started the book.'

'I don't know if it's the job itself, or just knowing you can't get off. But it does get to people. There was a man on the Brent Delta who filled his pockets with tools and threw himself off the side.'

'Why?'

'Who knows? People go from school to offshore, or from school to the army to offshore. They get everything done for them. They get institutionalised.'

'Are you?'

He reached around to knead the back of his neck, and frowned. It was a gesture already familiar to me, since Tom did it all the time.

'It's different for me,' he said. 'It took me a while to get offshore.'

He talked briefly about North Africa, though I got the impression he could have been moored anywhere. Oil is a country all of its own, a nation with moveable borders. Its frontiers are being pushed back all the time, into increasingly hostile territory. The age of easy acquisition is over. Every new prospect has problems, every windfall its own set of caveats. Matters of climate, geology, location, regime. Lack of infrastructure, intra-ethnic disputes, political wrangling over pipelines. Hostage-taking in Libya, piracy in West Africa, insurgents in Iraq, ice floes in Arctic Russia.

In the North Sea, the winter weather is rough, the seabed an impenetrable blend of shale and clay. In Brazil, the oil is locked under thick layers of salt. Central Asia somehow manages to combine the worst elements of every other petrostate: sour gas; civil unrest; banditry; oil buried deep at high pressure; frozen seas in winter, desert heat in summer, government intrigue all year round. In politically stable countries, the commute is a calculated risk, but most occupational hazards are confined to the rig: blow-outs, fires, condensate, chemical burns, heavy machinery, swinging loads. In more volatile regions, employees have to contend with the threat of kidnap, riots and terrorism, before they even get to work.

Extracting oil is a dirty, dangerous job. It is a pitched battle between human ingenuity, inhospitable terrain and highly combustible materials. The dangers are compounded by the locations' remoteness. Platforms store volumes of oil and gas on board, so the risk of explosion is always present. Rigs can, and do, sink, as in 1982, when the Ocean Ranger sank in Canadian waters, and 2001, when Petrobas 36, then the world's largest semi-submersible platform, capsized off the coast of Brazil. In 2010, Deepwater Horizon claimed eleven lives and became the largest marine oil spill in history. Disasters on this scale, though rare, serve to remind us how contingent our control is. After Deepwater Horizon, oil gushed into the Gulf of Mexico for three months. When Well 37 in Tengiz blew out, it burned for a year. It took Red Adair three weeks to extinguish Piper Alpha.

In the history of offshore exploration, there is no bleaker parable than Piper A. Known as 'the Monster', it was once the single largest oil producer in the world. By 1988, its best days were behind it. Piper Alpha had become known throughout the North Sea as a place where accidents happened. The year before, a rigger died there. On 6 July, the platform was undergoing essential maintenance. The asset holder, Occidental, considered stopping production while the work was carried out, but decided it would be too expensive.

What followed was a perfect storm of lax practice and poor conditions. It's referred to as the Swiss cheese model of causation. An organisation can layer its defences, but each layer will have a weak spot, like the hole in a slice of Emmental. When those holes line up, trouble finds its way in.

That day, a pressure valve was removed from a condensate pipe and replaced with a blind flange. There were problems with Occidental's permit system, and contractors didn't get proper training. When the night crew turned the alternate pipe on, they didn't know the valves had been swapped. The blind flange gave, and the gas leak triggered an explosion. The platform was built to store oil, not gas, so the walls could withstand fire, but collapsed before the first blast. The automatic deluge system had been switched to manual, because divers were working in the water near the pumps and there was a risk they could be sucked into the inlet. Oil from the neighbouring Tartan and Claymore platforms backed up down the pipeline, pumping fuel into the fire, even as men were abandoning the rig. They couldn't find anyone with the authority to stop production.

Soon, Piper Alpha was engulfed in flames that could be seen seventy miles away. One hundred and sixty-seven men died that night. Some obeyed their drill and retreated to the accommodation quarters. They were entombed inside when the platform buckled and the block slid into the sea. Others climbed to the helideck and waited to be saved. When it became clear no one was coming (within a minute of the first explosion, the helideck was enveloped in smoke, and the choppers couldn't get near), they had to save themselves by jumping into the sea fifty metres below. Those who didn't break their necks faced a choice: sink down into the dark and drown, or swim to the surface and burn. It is a tale of elemental fear. Raging fire. Burning sea. Survivors driven by the most basic instinct of all: to plant their feet back upon the earth.

For the sixty-one who escaped, the horror wasn't over. Some turned to drink. More than one committed suicide. Many suffered from PTSD, which was barely understood back then. Grown men in the north-east of Scotland didn't see therapists. When compensation was awarded, the ones able to articulate their grief got more than those too traumatised to talk. Survivor's guilt manifested itself in other, unsettling ways. One woman came home to find her husband standing at the bottom of a six-foot hole he'd impulsively dug in the garden. That man, Bill Barron, went on to model for Sue Jane Taylor, the artist who sculpted the Piper Alpha memorial in Hazlehead Park. The sculpture shows three figures, facing east, west and north, representing youth, physicality and oil respectively. I met Taylor once, and she walked me around the memorial garden, pointing out the rose plants chosen by the families of the dead, the long columns of names carved onto the sculpture's plinth.

Afterwards, we sat in the tearooms and watched the rain run down the windows, until the garden's green lineaments had all but disappeared and only the smeared pinks and reds of the rose beds were visible. She told me she had worked furiously on the memorial, never sure, until the very end, that there would be enough money to complete it. Together, the garden of remembrance and the sculpture cost £100,000. Of this, asset holders contributed £11,000. Occidental didn't want the memorial. The company thought the families ought to be satisfied with a book of condolence. In the days after the disaster, Occidental's head of PR went to see Taylor and tried to buy up every sketch, every photograph, every negative she had of the platform. He said she could name her price. She refused. Some artists can't be bought.

Occidental sold off its North Sea assets and braced itself for the inquiry. In the end, it paid out $100 million. Though the Cullen Report damned its safety procedures – and in doing so, transformed the culture offshore – no one person was ever found liable. North Sea standards are now the most stringent in the world, but there is still no way to rule out human error. If you ask people to work twelve-hour shifts, for twenty-one days, they will get tired and make mistakes. Accidents still happen, but many go unreported. They exist in an almost metaphysical realm: *If the media didn't hear about it, did it really occur?*

A few years ago, workers on the Magnus noticed an odd smell coming from the showers. Further investigation revealed the water supply to have been contaminated with diesel. BP issued guidelines. Workers were told to drink and clean their teeth with bottled water, yet continue to shower as normal. They might notice the 'harmless' scent of diesel, but should ignore it. It's worth noting here that BP also said Corexit, the dispersant it sprayed on the Gulf after Deepwater Horizon, was harmless, even as cleanup workers began to experience memory loss, muscle spasms and skin complaints, a set of symptoms last seen in Gulf War soldiers.

Procedures are designed to establish a chain of liability, so if something *does* go wrong it can be traced back to an individual. In reality, accidents are rarely one person's fault. Films like *Deepwater Horizon* feature villainous executives because it's difficult to dramatise corporate complacency and systemic failure. Piper Alpha came on the heels of Chernobyl, *Challenger* and the presciently named *Herald of Free Enterprise*. In some ways, it was a different time, an age of deregulation and ruinous misjudgment. But the story comes with a postscript that suggests lessons can be forgotten as quickly as they're learned.

On the twenty-fifth anniversary of the Piper Alpha disaster, a runaway train carrying Bakken Crude careered off the tracks at the town of Lac-Mégantic in Quebec, spilling six million litres of oil. As the oil ran into a storm drain, jets of flame exploded from pipes and sewers, setting the downtown area ablaze. Forty-seven people were killed; forty buildings destroyed. They tried to pin the blame on three rail workers. Instead, Canada's Transportation Safety Board exposed a company that cut corners and failed to train staff, while the government looked the other way. It was well established that the old tanker cars were not up to the job. And people who saw Bakken Crude come out of the ground described it as 'fizzy'. It has a high gas content, and is more flammable than heavy crude. Rail journeys can exacerbate this, shaking the oil around so the lighter gases rise to the surface. Yet these oil trains were routed through towns all over Canada and America, and no one bothered to tell residents about the nature of their freight.

It often feels as if safety is one more thing struck off the asset holder's to-do list and slipped on to the employee's. Offshore, they're encouraged to submit STOP cards, with details of any slip-up or safety lapse they might have witnessed. It's meant to empower people to speak up. More often, it encourages petty talebearing and pointless complaints, *aperçus* about colleagues who slouch in their chairs or neglect to put lids on their coffee. So strict are they about seemingly small points of safety – such as holding onto the handrail when going up and down a flight of stairs – that workers carry on observing them at home. Callum said he often found himself at the shops absent-mindedly clinging to the side of the escalator.

Before they even go offshore, employees have to complete a course in basic survival, the BOSIET. The certificate needs to be renewed every four years, and most first-timers fund it themselves. It's mainly undertaken to appease insurers. If your chopper ditches in the North Sea, it's unlikely you'll make it out alive. The odds of survival, slim in summer, are slashed again in winter, and the BOSIET does as much to ready you for the real thing as a flight attendant's pep talk prepares you for a plane crash. There is no way to replicate the conditions, though the old test was at least done in the sea. The test has since been moved inside, at the insistence of insurance companies.

Trainees are dressed in survival suits – the same eye-catching orange as DOC jumpsuits – and strapped into a simulator suspended over a swimming pool. The simulator is submerged and rolled over. Only when it stops turning can they unstrap themselves from their seats, kick the plastic windows from their brackets, and swim to the surface.

It sounds simple. It *is* simple, in theory. In practice, it is hard to harness a body in flight mode, to ignore its trilling panic. If you undo your belt too early, you will be catapulted upwards like an astronaut at zero gravity. The machine is built for men, so women, who make up around three per cent of the offshore workforce, will face further problems. A small woman will find it difficult to pull the belt tight enough and if a belt is loose it can flip around, so the buckle faces inwards. In normal circumstances, a twisted seatbelt is easy to fix. When you're tethered to your seat, upside down and underwater? Not so much.

Helicopter survival is the BOSIET's big-ticket event, the part everyone dreads, but not the only simulation on the course. Trainees are also sent into a simulacrum of a burning building. They once used real smoke, but insurers decided this too was dangerous. Now, you have to troop through a corridor filled with synthetic smoke, and feel your way out with the back of your hand. In the event of an explosion, when bulkheads are ripped apart and wiring exposed, you should never trail your palm along a wall. If the back of your hand brushes a live wire, the shock will knock you over. If your palm touches the wire, your hand will close around it. And you will cling on convulsively, until the voltage kills you.

★

Callum dropped us at the station after dinner. We stood on the platform, our breath coming out in plumes, as the train ticked beside us. It was a cold, pale evening, light as a lunch hour in London.

'When are you back?' Tom said.

'Friday.'

The carriage doors opened and closed with a pneumatic sigh. He put his bag down, and we hugged.

'He won't leave his wife, you know. They never do.'

'In this book,' I said, 'the man's first wife dies. She rolls her car on a pile of wet leaves on her way to see her lawyer. It's *very* sad.'

On the map, my hotel looked a manageable distance from town, but I'd not reckoned with the long queues of cars, and the agonising pace at which they crept across the river. Caden and I had argued again over where to stay. Couples, whatever their provenance, create their own customs, and this one was ours. He'd suggest an airport hotel, that his company would pay for. I'd argue for somewhere better, on the grounds that a cheap hotel would make our affair feel tawdry. The one holding the credit card won.

I'd won this time, but now felt a bit like an asset holder myself, haemorrhaging money on transport costs. We sat in gridlocked traffic, and the driver griped about business. The first question every passenger chirps as they slide into the back seat – *Been busy?* – unleashed a torrent of complaint. *No*, he had not been busy. Not since the oil price dropped, and companies had shifted workers onto a three-week rotation. The airport was empty. The men who managed to hang onto their jobs now caught the bus. The hotels and bars were deserted, the strippers chronically under-worked. Most of them spent their evenings on the doors, smoking and trying to catch passing trade.

To these tales of socio-economic woe, I added my own insights:

'*My* boyfriend thinks he'll be going three and three quite soon. *My* boyfriend says his company has cut everybody's pay by ten per cent. *My* boyfriend says there's nothing they can do about it, but he isn't very politicised. *My* boyfriend says his rig is half empty now, because they've fired so many people.'

'Which rig's your lad on?' he said, as we pulled up outside the hotel.

'Forties Echo,' I lied.

'Spent some time on there myself. I thought Apache had already gone three and three?'

'Well, *yes.*' I peered into the dark recesses of my bag, pretend-ing to look for my purse. 'But … that was just core crew. He's a contractor.'

'What did you say he did?'

When I looked up, he was frowning at me in the mirror. I offered him a guileless, closed-lip smile.

'My boyfriend is a pipe fitter,' I said.

I tried on four different outfits before he arrived. In the right light, my pale pink slut dress (christened thus because the mate-rial was thin, cheap, and cut very tight) looked sporty and youth-ful. Beneath the fluorescent strips in the bathroom, it looked desperate. Since turning thirty, I'd been subject to semi-regular crises of confidence, mostly to do with my face no longer match-ing my body. The slut dress's immediate antecedent was a short, stripy dress stolen from my sister. She had recently stolen it back, worn it to a baby shower, and stretched it out of all recognition. I put it on. The waistband sagged sadly. The white stripes were a dingy grey. I took it off and threw it on the floor. My favourite thing to wear was a black crepe jumpsuit with a high neck and peg trousers. I usually wore it with my Converse. Straight from the wash, the tight fit negated the prim neck and flat shoes. It looked sexy, and like I hadn't tried. But I'd worn it the last time we met; too recently for it to seem romantic. He'd just assume I had no other clothes. I put the leather leggings I'd been wearing all day back on. They were expensive, but every time I wore them, I was refreshed on their worth. After a day's wear, they still looked better than anything else in my case. I pulled on a grey marl T-shirt, better suited to someone who lived in a bin. This T-shirt wasn't new when I'd stolen it from a flatmate I disliked nine years ago. The sleeves were ragged, the neckline full of holes, but it had worn down to an abraded softness, and was the most comfortable piece of clothing I owned.

I brushed my hair, tied it back, and examined my reflection. The older I got, the less I could rely on it to behave. As the day wore on, my face moved through a series of sly and shifting iterations, so that I never knew who would greet me in the glass. Like a Rhys woman, I divided the world into the mirrors I looked nice in and mirrors I didn't. The former were losing ground all the time. I ordered a whisky from room service, and picked up a book. After reading the same paragraph several times, I put it down, and lined my lips with shaking hands. Tapped more freckles on my nose. Applied a fourth coat of mascara. A knock crashed outside. The wand veered, smearing purple across my eyelid. I cursed, and opened the door.

'Hello, you.'

It always took me a minute to process: the miracle of his face, an inch from mine. How unfeasibly *good* he looked. Early on, I couldn't remember him at all, seeing only a pixelated oval under a dark cap of hair. I couldn't look at his Instagram, since he wasn't allowed any social media in case he was tempted to contact other women. Even now, my memory of his face was uncertain. The Caden of my mind was coarser, less finely modelled than the real thing, so when I saw him, I experienced a moment's confusion as the twin versions floated in front of me, then reconfigured with a snap. Away from him, I allowed myself to think his appeal was subjective and strictly personal, something I'd discovered, the way an antiques dealer can detect the original lines of a piece beneath a clumsy veneer. Then I'd see him again, and remember. He was better than I gave him credit for.

'Did you get that beer from the bar?' I said. 'I told you to put it on the room.'

'I wouldn't *dare* do that.'

He put his hands on my shoulders and walked me backwards.

'I had the same driver as you. Think it was the same lad anyway. He asked me if I was meeting my girlfriend here, said he dropped you off before.'

I winced, remembering my lovesick prattling in the cab.

'I got you a present,' I said.

'What is it?'

'A book.'

I handed him a package. The copy of *Villages*, inexpertly wrapped. He looked down at it, deflated.

'I thought you could take it offshore with you. Although ...'

My fingers still gripped the parcel. Like most elder children, I struggled to share. In the banana republic of the playroom, I used to offer with one hand and snatch back with the other, requisitioning toys and books bestowed only minutes before. My sister's fury was the fury of the dispossessed. I took it in my stride. What did she expect? My things looked new again, once I'd given them away.

'Maybe it would be better if I hung onto it for now.'

'Why?'

'If you're not much of a reader, and you start bringing novels into the house, she might get suspicious.'

'Who says I'm not much of a reader?'

'*You.* You said you hadn't read a book in eighteen months.'

He shrugged, accepting the retracted gift as his due. We lay on the bed, drinking beer. He talked about work, offloading automatically, as people with desk jobs do every night. His new manager had complained about his communication, or lack thereof. I sympathised. By his own admission, he wasn't much of a talker.

'Tom's cousin told me a story before,' I said. 'About a man who filled his pockets with tools and threw himself off a rig.'

'On the Brent Field.'

'You know about it?'

'Aye. Everybody does.'

'What happened?'

He puffed out his cheeks, like a plumber confronted with a fulminating boiler.

'Fuck knows. I got told he had credit card debts.'

I took a sip of my beer and pushed my lips against his. Liquid foamed, and spilled down his chin. He swallowed and pulled away, swiping shyly at his mouth with the back of his hand.

'I love it when you do that. Is that weird?'

'No weirder than the impulse that leads me to do it in the first place.'

'Guess who turned up on our rig the other day?'

'Who?'

'That lad who called you a bad word. Jason.'

'You should have pushed him into the sea.'

'He got flown off. With an ear infection.'

'Good. I hope he goes deaf.'

His hair was shorter than I remembered, and shaved at the sides, like a boy soldier's. He pulled his top off, revealing the remnants of a tan on his back.

'Caden?'

'Hmm?' His voice, from behind the taut cotton, was muffled.

'You know when we had phone sex the other day?'

'Ye-es?'

'I was thinking we should try and recreate those conditions.'

'Shall I go sit on the landing, call you from there?'

After a brief struggle with his sleeves, he emerged. A cowlick at his temple stuck up, and out.

'You're like the girl in the poem. There was a little girl, with a little curl, right in the middle of her forrid ...'

'And when she was good, she was very, very good. And when she was bad, she was horrid.'

I reached up and smoothed it back down against his scalp.

'Bet you're horrid when you're bad. Aren't you?'

It wasn't bad. It was improved. Or was it? I couldn't tell. I loved him, and what is love but a temporary cessation of critical faculties? In certain respects, he was good in bed. He was generous with the duvet. He took up barely any room. It was nice that I could fall asleep on his chest. His body fit mine so snugly, it was as if he'd been modelled to my exact specifications. *Made for me*, I'd think, in those drifting moments before black. And I liked the way he turned his hands around, and ran the tipped edges of his fingers over my skin. It was a trick too subtle to be part of his own rough repertoire. A woman must have taught him that.

'Why are you so fit?' I breathed between kisses. 'Why are your arms so big?'

'Why are your eyes so big?' he countered, running his tongue over my clavicle. 'Why is your pussy so small? Why is your arse so fat?'

'Don't know.' I caught a hank of his hair in my fist, tipped his head back, tasted my sweat on his lips. 'Just the way I came out.'

Questions. There were more pressing matters than his arms, the whys and wherefores of their circumference. I didn't like to pry. To do so would be to refute the first rule of our little club of two. But on a long enough timeline, the chances of exposure rise thrillingly. When he wanted to see me, he blamed the sea state. But winter was thawing into spring, and summer's mists were not yet here. There was a reckless part of him that wanted to be caught.

'Where are you meant to be?'

'A course.'

'*What* course?'

'Confined space entry.'

I tutted.

'She won't check. She's got other things on her mind at the moment.'

'What things?'

I didn't want her to check, obviously, but I was still irritated by his dismissal of the possibility. It suggested I was beneath her notice, that she was orbiting above me, at a lordly level, occupied by matters realer and more urgent. Maybe she was. Maybe the shellac on her toenails was chipping faster than expected. Maybe her recently acquired calfskin tote was a half-tone darker than it looked in pictures.

'I'm going Vegas to see the fight. She's not happy.'

'What are you going to do?'

'Nothing I can do. I've booked the tickets now.'

He reached over me, for his beer.

'Who do you think will win? I watched the press conference the other night, and couldn't call it.'

It moved me to hear of his lonely vigils in front of the television. His wife went to bed at eight, like a medieval vassal, or a child, and though I knew it was possible he encouraged her early bedtimes, I couldn't help but picture him alone in the flickering light of the flat screen, like a small boy at a deserted matinee show. A married couple should watch television together. That was what people got married for, wasn't it? So they had someone to watch television with.

'I want to say Canelo.'

Caden sniffed.

'He's nowt but a ginger cheat.'

'You're one to talk.'

'Which round? I'll have a bet on whatever you say.'

Sweet, superstitious: the remote equivalent of asking me to blow on dice.

'Ninth. Stoppage. Kiss my neck.'

He kissed my neck; his fingers grazed my nipples.

'All Mexicans are cheats. See Margarito? He loaded his gloves.'

'He also got pasted in the rematch. Your sins will find you out.'

In the half-light, I could just about make out the tattoos on his arm. The sleeve was complex, expensive, full of incidental detail. It ran down over his right hand, like a gauntlet. The names of his wife and daughters were written in delicate cursive on his bicep. Below them, the instruments of man's ruin. A martini glass, filled with green liquid. Some scattered dice. A horseshoe. I traced the rim of the glass with my finger.

'You need a girl. In the glass, I mean.'

'I bought this painting a while back, with a lass in it. I wanted to get her, just there. But she'd go mad.'

'Why?'

'The woman in the painting has blonde hair. She's a redhead.'

'She'd be jealous of a drawing?'

'It's not worth the chew, finding out.'

His wife appeared at the foot of the bed. I could see her quite clearly, the way I could see certain characters in novels quite clearly. Her hair was the anaemic red of hot sauce, pulled into a bun so tight it looked painful.

'First night of our honeymoon, she asked us to come to bed. I wanted to stay in the bar, have another drink. When I got back to the room, she'd packed my case and ripped my coat into strips. She put the strips of the coat *on top* of the packed case.'

'She sounds like Ava Gardner.'

'How's that?'

'When she lost her temper, she couldn't find it for weeks.'

I was starting to associate his presence with lost sleep. The artificial chill of hotel rooms; the unyielding tension of the mattress. The practice of strapping two single beds together, tucking a sheet over the top and calling it a double. A subtle rift remained between the two. I kept finding myself wedged in the gap after reaching out for him, and rolling down into the declivity his body left behind.

I touched the glass again. The texture of his skin changed where it was tattooed. The ink made a granular ridge, like the rim of a real-life margarita, dipped in coarse salt.

'Some people are bottomless pits. You can give and give, but it will never be enough. You need a Vargas girl in that glass. It's like an icon, with no Madonna.'

'I'd like to get rid of the whole sleeve, but it's too far gone.'

He sighed, and shifted his weight. In the dark, I felt him run a hand over his arm.

'Sometimes I wish I could go back to the beginning. Start all over again.'

*

When I woke up, he was sitting on the edge of the bed. His hair was damp. There was a towel wrapped around his waist.

'What time is it?'

He pressed one finger on a slat of the blinds. Outside, the sky was white. People were going about the blameless business of their day.

'About nine. That's a guess, like.'

I sat up, and looped an arm around his neck. I put my lips against his shoulder.

'I'll miss you.'

'Caden told such dreadful lies ...'

'I don't lie to you.'

'It made one gasp and stretch one's eyes ...'

'Never to you.'

'His wife, who from her earliest youth, had kept a strict regard for truth …'

'I'm not *lying*.'

We lay down, his head resting on my stomach. I ran my palm over his hair. I thought I'd probably loved before, but this was different. This instinct to cling, to restrict his movement with my arms. *Tell me you love me*, I lobbied him in my head. *If you say it first, I'll say it back.*

'I need to ask you something,' he said.

My stomach flipped pleasantly. Only important questions needed a preface.

'Go ahead.'

He studied the coverlet. He was choosing his words. He was so nice. So sweet-natured, and thin-skinned. Alert to my every shift in mood, he'd sensed I needed something concrete, and soon. *Ask me if I love you*, I pressed him in silence. *Ask me and I'll say yes.*

'See when I go Vegas? Reckon I'll be the only white person at this Jay-Z thing?'

I rolled over onto my stomach and pressed my face into the pillow.

'What? Why are you laughing?'

I turned back over, and pushed my hair out of my face.

'You're so racist.'

'I'm not! I'm *not*. I just don't want to be the odd one out. Like a dot on a domino.'

I pressed the heels of my hands into my eyes.

'Even the imagery you're using to tell me you're not racist is racist.'

He was looking at me, unabashed but interested.

'Why?'

'It's like you're saying they're one big, black, undifferentiated … *mass*.'

'I bet I know more black people than you. You know we've got more asylum seekers in Stockton than anywhere else in the country? They dump them on us, because the property's cheap.'

For a moment, his smile sagged, and the brackets around his mouth reasserted themselves.

'And then they call us racist.'

*

As we went downstairs, his phone rang. He answered the call and walked away.

I assumed it was his wife, so dropped back. When I got into the taxi, I realised it was his back to back. Jobs offshore are split between two people; a back to back will be on the rig when you're home, and at home when you're away. In theory, you'll barely see this second self, but the two of you have to maintain close contact. They talked for a while, about a leak that had sprung the night before. One or both of them would be blamed. The platform was ageing badly. Bits of it seemed to break down or fall off with alarming regularity. He reached for my hand as he talked, in mute apology. I watched the rocky outcrops and banks of rain-soaked vegetation flow past. He ended the call on the outskirts of Dyce, where we sat snarled in gridlocked traffic. How did people survive, in a place of such overwhelming drabness? Everything was grey. The sea, the sky, the houses, the dry stone walls that divided the sloping fields of cows.

'Your pupils are like pinpricks,' I said. 'Have you been taking smack?'

He placed my hand against his lips. 'Something like that.'

It was crew change day. Men in grey tracksuits swarmed through the airport.

He queued to collect his boarding pass, and I stood near the exit, watching them walk out to the rank. They had a questing look about them; country lads off to seek their fortune, kit bags slung over their shoulders like bindles. In the eighties, they called them Thatcher's children. In reality, they were more like Thatcher's wards. Men from despised boroughs and voided northern towns. Tracts of managed decline and dying industry. Teesside, Wearside, Tyneside, Durham. Doncaster, Oldham, Hartlepool, Hull. Union reps stood outside the heliport, trying to persuade people to sign up, but trade unions weren't trusted offshore. Though it was part of the north-east's catechism to hate Thatcher and all she stood for, the pioneer spirit that saw them shift their working lives out to sea had something in common with the buccaneering ethos of Thatcherism itself.

We walked to passport control. Four men stopped in front of us. Caden greeted them without embarrassment. I lagged behind, like a surrendered wife.

'How was Flamingo Land?' said one.

'Shite,' said Caden blandly. 'I was too small to get on any of the rides.'

I turned to look at the man who'd spoken. He looked back at me. His look said he knew all of my secrets, and found them unedifying.

'Who's this then, lad? Your eldest?'

The others laughed.

'Didn't like *that*, did she?' said another.

We went around the corner, out of sight. I could feel the malevolent force of the men at my back. I wished I'd let him come alone.

'They were rude.'

He glanced over my shoulder.

'I told you. The rules are different offshore.'

'They knew a lot about you. They seemed like gossips.'

'They are gossips. But it won't go no further than the rig.'

'They'll go round saying you're a gallis.'

'What's a gallis?'

My idiom was porous. Some south London had leached in. Where had I picked up *gallis*? A snippet of MC's chat from an old garage set floated back to me: *This one's for the gallis, the man dem who got more than one girlfriend*. Literally, a corruption of *girl-ist*. A man versed in the black art of philandering. An expert in the field of pussy.

'What if this gets back to your wife?'

I searched his face for a trace of concern. How would I have dealt with this, if our positions were reversed? Full crisis management mode, no doubt. Get ahead of the story with my own version of events, fashioned from the raw materials of fact. A breezy phone call to my husband once I was through passport control, just to let him know I'd slept well, was at the airport now and – *oh, guess what* – had bumped into someone I knew at arrivals, who happened to be on the same flight.

'I should go,' I said. 'It's terrible luck to watch a person leave.'

'I'm going to miss you, beautiful.'

He tugged at the collar of my coat, but it was no good. Despair had put down roots in me. This was us, this was our natural habitat. Airport lounges, hotel rooms. Zones of transit and delay, where the rubric of real life was suspended.

'You're such a liar. You're as bad as Owen in *Villages*.'

His hand moved up, and made contact with the skin above my collar. He pulled me close. Close enough that I could account for each dark lash, each pale freckle on his cheek.

'True story,' he said.

It's no as bad as prison. Anyone who's telling you it's like prison has no been to prison. I did three months in Colchester. I was in the Marines, but got chopped out. I got into a set-to with my commanding officer. I knocked him out, broke his jaw. I was already on my third court martial. I have a problem with authority. Did I have a bad relationship with my father? No. Wait a minute. Yes! Sort of. My mum and dad split up when I was ten. I didn't speak to him for seven years.

THREE

TIFFANY

'Are they still here?' I asked.

The letting agent turned his candid gaze upon me.

'Oh *no*. That was a long time ago. This area has become very fashionable.'

Fashionable! As if any part of Aberdeen could claim to be in vogue.

'My friend told me this was the red light district.'

'Your friend is working off old information. The only thing that will keep you up at night here is the seagulls.'

I'd already settled on the flat, for the irrational reason that I liked this man. He was in his fifties, blue-eyed and neatly bearded, with the urbane good looks of an ageing game show host. He drove me around the city in a sapphire-coloured BMW and talked about a series of crime novels he liked. Had I read any of them? No, I said. Oh you must, he said. They're *very* good. I will, I promised happily. I'll make it my first order of business when I get home.

'No,' he said, moving over to the window. 'This, *this* is where you want to be. Right in the thick of things.'

I followed him. The flat overlooked a car park at the back, a small building yard at the front. Unseen around the corner, but unmistakably there: the sea. Its salt proximity could always be felt, even when it was out of sight. A seagull the size of a lap dog landed on the window ledge. Cold eyes. A caustic yellow, the colour of hazard.

'Pity you can't see the water from here,' I said.

'Ah. A sea view. But for that, you're talking another three hundred a month.'

He smiled, exhilarated by the thought of saving money. Louisiana avarice and Protestant thrift, that's what Aberdeen was made of. If the city was rich – buffered from the worst excesses of the recession, an enclave of full employment and low crime – its wealth was largely invisible. No one knew where the black billions had gone, but they hadn't trickled down to the infrastructure. The centre was grey and functional, the roads congested at all times of day. The sea ran right into town, and sat there, unremarked. Yellow supply boats waited in rows against the sea wall. Beyond that, there was just empty water and the subtle streaking of the northern sky. Norway. Everyone here spoke breathlessly of the Norwegian sector. A sovereign wealth fund. The Statoil dream. It wasn't the principle of nationalisation they liked, the high industry standards it bought, or the generous public provision. It was accrual for accrual's sake. All that lovely money, stacking up. A pot of capital, swelling voluptuously, like rice in milk.

People compared Norway to a drug dealer who fastidiously eschews his own product. The country exported huge amounts of crude, yet relied on green energy itself. Over the water, they called it *oljeeventyr* – the oil fairy tale – and it really was. A million krone in the bank for every citizen, rigs that looked like hotels, fields with names like Troll, Valhall, Frigg.

Of course, there was a levy on its good fortune. There always is, in fairy tales. Oil turned the Norwegians shiftless and spoiled. They took three-day weekends, and ran up personal debt. They scuttled out of the office at four and shipped in Swedes to do their bar work. There was even a new verb, 'to Nav', or extract benefits from the state. Their government had bought them the latitude to be lazy. The Norwegian homily always ended with the same words: 'They started that oil fund in the nineties, and they're *only just dipping into it now.*' Consider our own North Sea story, a sorry tale of Thatcherite profligacy. We didn't save our windfall. We earned it and burned it. On what, no one seems sure. Fifty years since the first well was drilled, and we have nothing to show for our oil. And they say socialists don't know how to manage money.

'I don't care about a sea view that much,' I said. 'How much is it?'

'Eight hundred.'

I ran my finger along the window ledge. There was a fine coating of dust on the paintwork. People were clearing out; the downturn had seen to that. I should probably try to negotiate a better price – six months' rent here would take most of my savings – but I found that kind of conversation difficult. I took a hands-off approach to money, like the Queen. It had been Adam's métier, when we were together, since he cared about it more. The day I went to fetch my things from his flat, he thrust some pictures of a house he'd just bought towards me. 'This could have been yours,' he said grandly, as if sharing the deeds to Pemberley, rather than an unexceptional end terrace in Catford. 'Everything I own could have been yours.' 'And doesn't it say it all,' I replied, wrapping my one good coat in tissue paper, 'that I'd rather be doing this?'

I turned back to the letting agent.

'I'll take it,' I said.

He beamed at me. I had given the correct answer.

'I thought you might say that.'

He handed me some papers, and stood over me as I signed them. He reminded me of my friend Ali Andrews, whom I could imagine ageing in the same lean, finely incised way. He shared Ali's slightly disconcerting habit of bouncing forward on his toes when he wanted to emphasise a point. Ali was the first person I'd ever known to work offshore. Also: the source of my (possibly erroneous) conviction that all offshore workers were fit, even when they weren't, like firemen. It was a sign. I knew it.

Signs; portents. I was more alive to them than I used to be.

When I showered in the morning, I wrote Caden's initials, then mine, in the condensation on the glass. CD. TL. Then I drew a circle around them, so they were bound together.

I put perfume of tuberose and amber in my hair. I waited four minutes exactly before answering his texts.

I slept in a T-shirt turned inside out for luck (and gave account to other superstitions: when a person appears in your dream, he went to sleep thinking of you; if a man is quiet, but talks quickly, it means he can keep secrets).

Daily, I drilled him on the worst-case scenario. Wipe your texts every time we talk. Leave your phone out where she can see it. No new clothes to go offshore, no smashing the gym before you leave. And if she does catch you, please don't say *it was just sex*. But equally, don't tell her I was special. She will ask if I'm prettier than her, if I'm younger than her, if I let you do the things to me she won't let you do to her (these are trick questions, to which there are no right answers). She will want to know what my cunt tastes like, if I swallowed, if you put it in my arse. Don't be surprised if she wants to fuck after you tell her these things, if she fucks you harder, more desperately, than she's ever fucked before. Don't think this gets you off the hook.

Caden didn't seem to care about his wife. Or else, he couldn't picture being caught. So I added her to my private roster of fears. I thought if I fretted for both of us, she might never find out.

When I gave my notice in at work, my editor told me she'd miss me, then had a long conversation with another editor, over the top of my head, about the unlikelihood of attracting a decent replacement, given my simian day rate. Up until that point, I'd thought walking out of a job might be one of those decisions I'd come to regret. After that day, I stopped worrying.

On my last day, one of the directors took me out for lunch. I hovered in the doorway of her office as she finished a phone call. There was a framed poster on the wall behind her. It said: *Everything will be OK in the end. If it's not OK, it's not the end.*

We walked down to a tapas restaurant on The Strand. Inside was like a cool, dark cave. I picked at morcilla and salt cod while she pressed me about my plans.

'You should write a thriller. That's what's selling at the moment: thrillers by young women. How old are you?'

'Thirty-three.'

'There's no chance you might work things out with your ex?'

I shook my head. I didn't want to talk about my old boyfriend. I wanted to talk about my new boyfriend, though decorum prevented me from doing so.

She considered me, her head on one side.

'After a certain point, you *do* have to recalibrate your expectations. I know several girls who ended up married to men they turned down in their twenties. Nice, solid, dependable guys. You need someone who can be a friend, first and foremost.'

I looked past her, at the sluggish lines of lunchtime traffic converging on Trafalgar Square. I'd pictured this going differently. I'd admired this woman for years. I'd wanted to get her alone, because I thought she might have something useful to impart.

'I have to say,' she continued, 'I think you're very brave. Dating at your age is so hard. Men will assume you're desperate for a baby. The good news is, it gets easier again after forty, because they all think you're past it.'

I took a long swallow of sangria.

'Every cloud,' I said.

At the office, they gave me a bottle of champagne and a mocked-up magazine cover, *per* tradition. My head grafted onto a model's body, surrounded by slyly referential headlines. I thought I recognised Tom's snide style in a few, such as 'Ruffneck Ting: How To Get Drilled On An Oil Rig'. My editor had tears in her eyes as she gave a short, decorous speech that somehow made it sound as if the two of us had never met, and the people gathered at my desk all clapped.

I clutched my bouquet of goodbye roses to my breast, inclined my head and smiled, superb as a prima donna on her fifteenth curtain call.

Back at my mother's house, I found my sister already installed. Boo Boo, her ragdoll cat, was also *in situ*. Boo Boo was overbred, and too foolish to go outside. He had fat white legs, balanced on fine blue feet, so he looked like he was wearing gaucho pants tucked into blue boots. His USP was that he sagged, as if injected with morphine, when he was picked up, though he didn't have a docile temperament. He scared easily, and bolted at the smallest noise, running off with a bustling, short-legged stride. I suspected this was phase one of a long-term plan to dump Boo Boo on our mother, a suspicion confirmed when my sister told me he'd be there until August. 'My mum says she'll have him,' she said. 'Just while the kitchen gets done.'

In conversation, my sister and I tended to refer to our mother as 'my mum' rather than just 'mum', which made us sound both mildly possessive, and like we weren't related. I didn't fully understand her reasons for being there and didn't much care, since her presence mandated mine, and made me feel less like a spinster daughter. My sister *did* care about my movements, though. Along with the more obvious symptoms of her condition, I'd noticed an increased beadiness about her. There was probably an evolutionary explanation for this (the expectant mother's enhanced instincts; a desire to exert control over her surroundings), but in the relatively safe confines of our mother's house, it expressed itself as an extreme interest in my comings and goings.

In between peering at sludge-coloured swatches and saying 'Mouse's Back' and 'Elephant's Breath' over and over again, until the words seemed to lose all meaning, she asked questions, and pulled faces at the replies. She liked to look over my shoulder at my phone, and barge into the spare bedroom without knocking. If I said yes to a second glass of wine at dinner, she'd raise an eyebrow and say, 'Getting on it, are we?'

'Who's *Caden?*' she said one evening. 'That's not a proper name.'

'When did you get so nosy?' I said, putting my phone back in my pocket. 'I thought pregnant women were meant to be absorbed by their condition.'

'Are we going?'

My father called out from his bed. He lived in a nursing home a few miles from our mother's house, and had been bed bound several years. My sister fiddled with the console on the bed frame. The gradient of his mattress could be elevated at the press of a button, both the head and the foot, a move that always put me in mind of those bouncing Chevy Impalas in old rap videos. My father sailed up, down, up, down. She left him at an obtuse angle that looked uncomfortable, but meant he could see the television. It was stuck on an old episode of *The Great British Bake Off*. The remote often went missing, and the orderlies had taken to hiding it in his wardrobe. They blamed the other residents, who were still mobile, and sometimes wandered into his room and stole things.

'I don't like Paul Hollywood,' I said. 'He looks like the kind of man who'd make you do degrading things in bed.'

'*I* wouldn't know,' my sister said.

She pressed her lips together. It was only a day since she'd made one of her unscheduled appearances in my room and caught me opening a parcel from Myla. The underwear – pale blue, diaphanous, with strategic cutaways – was not really underwear but lingerie, the sort worn to be taken off.

'Shall we go?' my father suggested.

A woman appeared at the child gate, rattling at the catch. She must have been very new, because she was still bright-eyed, plump and hale. After a few weeks, residents all looked the same. Their skin took on a greyish cast, their eyes went dull, and they started to lurch about with a sleepwalker's gait. Most fictional sub-species have their roots in real illness. Vampires probably had porphyria; werewolves were likely rabid. Was this where zombies came from, I'd think, as they trundled past his room, moaning softly to themselves, occasionally stopping to worry at the gate. There was a laminated sign on the fire door leading to the car park, adjuring people to *CHECK* that visitors were visitors before letting them out, but it wasn't necessary.

'Hi there!' the woman said, as our eyes met. 'Haven't seen you for *absolutely ages*.'

My sister smirked.

'You didn't tell me you had a mate in here.'

It was obvious she had me confused with someone else, someone from her past, but I felt a guilty pang all the same. I didn't go
and see my father as much as I should. When I did, I tried to time
it so that my sister was there too. Back when he had preferences,
she was his favourite child, so I thought it only fair she should do
the heavy lifting of our visits. Conversation with him was difficult, since he could no longer think clearly or speak distinctly. His
personality had been voided, swapped for a collection of symptoms and some half-remembered imperatives. As a younger man,
he was outdoorsy, always dragging us off to empty tracts of
countryside for picnics and long walks, the sole purpose of which
appeared to be refreshing us on how good we had it back in our
bedrooms. He wanted, at one point, to move us all out to the
Highlands, but our mother told him to forget it. He used to stand
by the door with his coat zipped up, bristling with irritation, as we
hunted for lost shoes, hair bobbles, rain macs, gloves. Now, illness
had consigned him to a perpetual lobby, where he was doomed
to wait (coat on, eager to go) as his slow-moving family failed to
mobilise.

In effect, we had three fathers. The invalid, the laconic man I
thought of as our 'real' father, and the father of our mother's
stories, my least favourite of the three. This father was a soggily
constant figure, much given to battling his way through snow-
storms / race riots / forest fires, to deliver our mother a cup of clear
soup / rose gold regard ring / four-page love letter. She liked to pull
these stories out the bag whenever one of my boyfriends was
wavering, or engaged in some act of high selfishness. It wasn't
clear whether they were meant to make me envious or inspire me
to raise my standards, though in fact, they did neither.

I didn't want a man who would get the train to Wrexham with
me, then go straight home, because he thought me too precious

to sit in a carriage by myself. Besides, I didn't believe in this version of my father. He bore no resemblance to the terse, cross person I knew, whose black moods were so pervasive I could tell what kind of day he'd had from the sound of his key in the lock. As a teenager, I used to wish he'd leave us. I envisaged our family, minus his temper, as a harmonious unit of three. Now he had left us, and we were, for the most part, harmonious, though his leave-taking came with its own complications.

For one thing, our mother was hoarding again, stockpiling old biros and receipts and plastic ramekins and empty shampoo bottles. The kitchen looked like a vanitas painting, full of rotting fruit and bits of old food, and I thought there *was* an element of instruction to these little vignettes, a Calvinist rationale at play. To her, it was sinful to discard a bottle of shampoo before diluting the dregs with warm water, or to chuck a receipt in the bin without first recording the transaction in a lined notebook marked 'accounts'. My sister said it was a response to the trauma of my father's illness. I thought it was equally likely that living alone had freed her up to indulge her true passion. My father had been a tidy man, who enjoyed spending money.

Sometimes, I worried she was slipping into parallel vagueness. Nothing showy or dramatic – *petit mal*, as compared to his grand lunacy – but enough to give me pause. Confusing the television with real life used to be his department, but one night she suggested I go out with Robert Peston. 'She doesn't know Robert Peston,' my sister said. 'How would she ask him out?' My mother replied that his wife was dead, and he was on the scene. She'd heard him talking about it on Radio 4. Tinder didn't appeal, apparently. He wanted to meet his next wife in a naturalistic setting.

I watched this exchange in silence. Since the burglary, my life had taken on an air of spectacle, a performance piece my family felt obliged to look at, and comment on.

'Are we right?' my father said.

We took this as our cue to go. I kissed my father, and told him I'd be away for six months. Why I offered a timeline to a person for whom time no longer had any meaning, I'm not sure. He looked at me, his mouth slack, his black eyes communicating their own message. That he too was absent, and would be gone for some time.

'Hang on,' he said. 'I'm coming with you now.'

★

When I got to Aberdeen, I shopped for two days. Two winter-weight duvets, eight pillows, linen with an unobtrusive pale blue motif. Felt coat hangers, the same vague blue. A light wool throw; a cushion printed with a dog's face, in lieu of an actual dog. White cups, white plates. Red roses, heavily scented. Painted mugs in the shape of swollen-bellied birds. I bought cheap crockery, so I could spend more on towels. Rose Otto bath oil. Sugar scrub. I bought cheese, pâté, beer, wine, bitter leaves, a brown loaf. I went to Morrisons on King Street for a knife and a chopping board, and had a sudden sense of what I must look like to the other customers. A whey-faced woman in her thirties, spending Saturday night alone, buying kitchen utensils cheap enough to shame a student. A battered wife. An asylum seeker. Witness to some violent crime, relocated by a silent arm of government, her new address designated by algorithm.

When I finished, I poured myself a glass of wine and considered my work. The flat was high up, like an eyrie. Coastal light streamed in and bounced off the white walls and the white linen. Despite my best efforts, the rooms remained blank, as featureless as the bedroom of a budget hotel, or a doctor's waiting room. I felt then that I had failed. A proper woman, the sort who aspired to marriage and family life, would have been able to make an impression on the rooms. She would have left an imprint. Perhaps I should have bought some of those decorative wooden letters, the ones that declare windowsills and bookshelves to be HOME.

It was April and still cold. Some mornings, there were panels of frost on the windows. 'We had snow last week,' people kept saying. 'You just missed it.' They spoke sympathetically, as if I'd missed something nice. They were proud of their city's mad, unseasonal weather, the way it pivoted from squalls, to sun, to rain, then back to sun again.

The climate of my block was changeable too, hot and cold, light and dark, depending on whether a cruise ship was docked or not. These liners were vast, out of all scale to the slant streets they docked next to. They threw the surrounding area into darkness, and made cool gullies of the pavement below, like the sectors of sidewalk beside skyscrapers. I'd walk through their shadows, pulling my coat tightly round me. Then they'd sail away, and sunlight would flow through the streets again.

Friends called from London. 'What are you *doing* all day?' they asked. *Nothing* was the honest answer, though I could hardly tell them that. Discipline is a muscle and mine was beginning to waste. The days stretched before me, long and formless. I thought idly about my book, and took myself shopping. I got my nails done and my hair fixed, as if I were my own kept wife. I gave myself new names. When I bought coffee, I'd say it was for Hadley (*H-a-d-l-e-y*, I'd sing out, with pre-emptive clarity). When I ordered taxis, I'd say they were for Saskia. On Tinder, I was Elodie.

I told Caden Tinder was research. And it was true that I was only speaking to men who worked offshore. That this made me no different from most women in the city was somehow beside the point. Aberdeen Princess Syndrome. That's what locals called it. A congenital condition, passed from father to daughter, as most mutations are. Daddy was big in oil, so boyfriends had to be too. Late-stage symptoms included Longchamp bags, swinging tails of pastel-coloured hair, and a delicate hauteur when dealing with men in bars. These girls had no problem accepting a tray of cocktails, then sending the chancing cunt on his way. I'd seen it happen more than once.

Aberdeen was like a Gulf state, a desert caliphate. Women were rarely seen out alone after dark. It was full of itinerant workers, miles from home and lonely. Every few minutes, my phone lit up with messages from men. Canadian men, Polish men, French men, Nigerian men. Shy men and conceited men. Men who asked diffident questions about my work. Men who sent unsolicited pictures of their dicks. Men who got pettish if I took too long to respond. Men whose fitful patterns of communication made me think there was a girlfriend lurking stage left. Men who sought to differentiate themselves with zingy one-liners. Men who could barely string a *hi how r u?* together.

Like a brunette Goldilocks, I sifted through them, and found the majority wanting. This one's freckles are distributed unevenly, this one's eyelashes are too sparse. This one is wearing red chinos, but this one uses the word *party* as a verb. This one says *u* instead of *you*, the insignia of a moron, but this one's punctuation is too precious. This one is posing with his car so he'll be unreconstructed and money-grubbing. But *this* one is wearing a polo neck so he'll be effete. This one mentions his daughter in the first line of his profile, which seems aggressively parental. But this one has redacted his son's face with marker pen, and that's just creepy. Your name sounds French, they'd say to me. You look French, too. Are you French? Yes, I'd tell them. I am French. I'm from Nîmes.

They all asked how long I'd been single. It was code for *What's the matter with you?* Too long on the market meant commitment issues, grave personal shortcomings, or both. Not long enough meant insecurity, an inability to be alone, possible overlap. In London, it was just about possible that an unclaimed man of thirty-four was normal. In the provinces, it hinted at an intractable defect of character. I'd eye men released at this late stage with suspicion, more so if they were attractive and in full employment. *Why*, I'd think, *are you single? What species of damage did you do, that a grown woman wanted rid of you?* I dealt with this problem by deploying the methods of ageing bachelors everywhere: I filtered out anyone over twenty-nine. This too had its drawbacks. Young men in real life were more like the young men on television than I'd expected. They shared their vanities and preoccupations. They watched their carbs, went to the gym every day, spurned socks, took lots of pictures of themselves. They wanted to talk on text for hours, exchanging such volumes of information that meeting in person felt faintly pointless.

Much of my time was taken up with Caden, who kept calling, with the same questions as my friends. What *exactly* was I doing? And where was I, and with whom? I put this down to vicarious interest, an attempt to escape the sameness of his days.

He couldn't understand why I wanted to write about offshore. In his opinion, it was boring. He had mates who served in the military, and they said it was basically the same, except offshore you had more autonomy. It was like the army, with the moral dimension stripped out: no one cared about your character if you got the job done. The chain of command was analogous to the navy's, with the Offshore Installation Manager (OIM) serving as the captain of the rig.

The atmosphere was somewhere between a prison and a school. Cliques formed in the canteen. Some lads had history, grudges and bad blood going back years. If you worked on a building site, issues could be settled with a fight, but anyone caught fighting on a rig would be removed, so feuds ran on and on, unresolved. A lot of the old camaraderie was gone. In the eighties, tensions that built up during the day could be worked out in the evenings over a game of darts or pool. If you had a fight with your wife, you discussed it with your colleagues. It was known as the tea shack surgery. Now, everyone was glued to their devices, and scuttled straight to their rooms after their shift. They were surrounded, but atomised. Twenty years ago, asset holders put televisions in the cabins. It was a slick corporate move, masquerading as a gift.

People on drill rigs had it somewhat easier. They had one job, one objective: to drill holes. A production platform was like an ecosystem. It had to sustain several separate groups competing for the same resources. There were teams of contractors and sub-contractors, with clashing cultures and separate agendas, coming and going all the time. There was one rule for the company men, another for everyone else. And there was downward pressure from the asset holder, because oil companies only care about one thing: production.

But it was the monotony, rather than the stress, that bothered Caden. Every day was the same. He woke up at six, to start his shift at seven. A rig runs twenty-four hours a day, its days split into two twelve-hour shifts, which are in turn split into smaller segments. They got an hour for their dinner, breaks in the morning and afternoon, and a few short 'in-betweenies'. Everything was done for them – meals cooked, beds changed, clothes laundered, cabins cleaned – so after work, there wasn't much to do. He usually went to the gym, then retired to his cabin to watch box sets, before going to sleep at ten.

'*Which* box sets?' I said one night, hoping to catch him out.

'*Breaking Bad*,' he replied smoothly. 'Though I'm liking *The Wire*.'

'Where are you up to?'

'Brother Mazoune's just been shot. Have you got me a burner yet?'

He'd taken several seasons back with him, and had become obsessed with acquiring a burner. *Graft phones.* That's what they called them in Liverpool. A misnomer, for she was the graft, not me. Usually the girlfriend is shunted onto the graft phone while the wife retains the rights to the registered number, but the old order was collapsing.

'It's on my list.'

'What are you doing?'

'Watching *Grand Designs.* I don't know why. Everyone on it has too much money.'

Kevin McCloud was frozen on my laptop's screen, mid-remonstration with a couple wearing matching Barbours. Pertly, they faced him down with the blithe conceit of the moderately moneyed. They reminded me of Adam's parents. I wished a hex on them, on their dream home and their arrogant plans to be in by midwinter.

'I'm watching the football. They all rich bastards too.'

'At least you know why they're rich. The people on *Grand Designs* are all rich for unsaid, mysterious reasons. They should make them disclose their tax returns at the beginning.'

'Do you miss me?'

There was a plaintive note in his voice that wasn't usually there. I sounded different too. I was speaking in my normal voice. More often, I used a babylike coo on him, based on Jennifer Lopez's chewy contralto in the opening seconds of *Love Don't Cost a Thing* (You're not going to be able to make it? *Again?*).

'Of course.'

'I hate you going out with other lads. It gives me a knot in my stomach.'

'It's only research.'

'*I* was research. Look what happened there.'

'That's different.'

There was a definite change in his personality when he was offshore. He became clingier, and desperate for contact. He wanted to speak to me first thing in the morning, then at midday, then again in the evening. If I didn't reply to his texts within the hour, he was thrown into crisis.

'I'm going to tell my mam tomorrow. About you.'

'What *for*?'

'I need to talk to someone. My head's busting with all this stuff.'

'I can't believe I even need to say this, but you *cannot* tell your mother.'

'Who can I tell then?'

'No one!'

'You've told people.'

'I'm not married.'

'My mam isn't like yours. She doesn't come back with opinions.'

'So what's the point of telling her?'

He was annoying me. I wanted to tip him upside down and shake him until two words of sense fell from his lips, to haul him in front of a truth and reconciliation commission so they could do the legwork for me. He was silent for a minute.

I was learning the lexicon of his silences. He was either upset, or had run out of stuff to say. I heard the chime of the tannoy in the background, a male voice frayed by static.

'I'm freezing,' I said. 'I think I'm coming down with something.'

'I wish I was there to look after you.'

'I'm going to get a bath.'

'Send us a picture.'

I looked out of the window. The rain was falling in sheets, onto the car park, the cobbled street, the corrugated roof of the building yard lockup. *I'm not going out there*, I thought. *It's too wet.*

'I can't.'

'Please,' he wheedled. 'It's shite, being out here three weeks. I thought I'd be able to handle it, and I can't. I need something to keep me going.'

'I don't feel sorry for you. You should have joined your union.'

I never dreamt it would be so difficult to get a decent picture of my breasts. Every time I found an angle that showed them looking firm and youthful, half my face encroached on the frame, double-chinned and – seen from below – unfairly haggard. A photo in profile, which helpfully cropped out my head, included the obdurate swell of my stomach. Blinds up, the grey light cast an unflattering render on my skin. Blinds down, it was too dark to see anything. Taken from the front, elbows pressed inwards to slim my waist, my breasts had the pendulous aspect of a nursing ape's. Taken from above, as I lay on the bed, they looked flat and splayed. I turned this way and that. I struggled to press the button while keeping the phone steady.

I swore and gave up, several times. Then, suddenly, on the ninety-fourth attempt, there it was. The breasts high and heavy at once, a deep brown juncture between them, curving shadows below, giving them a silken heft they didn't have in real life. The nipples so dark and large I could be pregnant. The silver cross – the same one he readjusted the first time he kissed me – glinting below my collarbone. There was an ochre cast to the photo, like an oil painting. The body (artfully cut off at the neck; I'd written too many articles about revenge porn not to) didn't look like mine. It looked good. Even through the baleful lens of female self-assessment, I could see that. Perhaps this is the secret to all successful acquisition. Just stay the course; keep going.

This occurred to me later on, as I was lying in bed. The rain was still falling, and the flat was cold. For the first time I felt lonely, and wished I could go home.

I was almost asleep when my phone lit up, throwing a dim blue oblong against the wall.

What do u think about us being properly together???

The treble question mark. Caden's way of denoting an important question. There was a fluttering in my stomach: pleasure, panic. I wrote *Ok* and put the phone down. As I did, it lit up again.

Are u sure??? Obviously, I do come with baggage.

Didn't he just. Typing quickly, too quickly to consider the consequences, I wrote:

Yes. I'm sure.

When you get home, you've got a lot of steam to let off. Women don't tend to understand that. Well, naw. It's not that they don't understand. They just don't fucking like it. All of a sudden you've got this really drunk guy, who appears slavering shite, probably wanting sex, probably incapable of sex, and it really annoys them. It's like: 'Oh, I was looking forward to you coming home, I thought we could have a nice romantic night'. But you just need that one big blowout.

FOUR

T-211

'Where's he from?'

It was breakfast time in Las Vegas, and Caden was slurring already.

'Erm ...' I gathered up my keys and my purse, dropped them into my bag, and felt a blankness descend on my brain. Where did this myth *come* from, that women were good at doing two things at once? 'Here, I think.'

'What did you say his name was?'

'Said.'

'Si-*eed*? Don't sound like he's from here.'

'What do you care?'

'Men aren't on there to find a lass. The lads at work say it's nowt but slags.'

'So what? Your rig's hardly a cradle of gender equality. Your colleagues aren't representative of the entire population.'

I spoke with more conviction than I felt. Caden liked to convey gloomy stories back from the rig, and my secret fear was that his colleagues *were* representative of the entire population, that all men were like this, all the time.

'Anyway, we're just friends.'

'Men don't want girls for mates. Not up here. That's a London thing.'

Like a bizarro Scott Garcia, Caden classed much of what I did as 'a London thing', and as such, outside the realms of normal. Pursuing friendships with the opposite sex; drinking wine; eating fish without a cladding of batter; trying to pay for dinner or a round of drinks; exercising my right to vote. All were aberrant habits I'd picked up in the capital. He disavowed everything to do with the city (the noise, the numbers, the immigrants, even the smog, which I thought a bit rich, coming from him). If it ever came up in conversation, he dismissed it with stern brevity: *That's not for me.*

'He's very civilised. He's a driller.'

'He'll be overpaid, then. Don't buy no drinks.'

'Are you having a nice time?'

'No,' he said indifferently. 'It's too hot. You've got to pay a grand to sit down. They wouldn't let us into that Jay-Z thing. Said I was too drunk. She's not speaking to us, neither. I rang before. She called us a selfish cunt and put the phone down.'

'You did leave it four days to call. She probably thought you were lying in a pile of wreckage at the bottom of the sea.'

'She wouldn't care,' he intoned. 'She hates me.'

I disliked Caden's habit of referring to his wife as 'she'. It made her seem omnipotent, and created confusion when there was more than one woman in the story.

'What are you wearing?' he said.

'The slut dress.'

I was actually dressed in a navy blue jumpsuit, with military details, like something Janet Jackson might have worn on her Rhythm Nation tour. And trainers, for proper dancing. *Trainers for Proper Dancing.* The working title of my stolen book! I wanted my book back, and knew there was no chance of that. Larceny is a fact of life, like taxes. We thieve, and are victims of theft too. Grownups should be able to accept this.

'Send us a picture.'

'I'm late. I don't have time to fuck about filtering my tits.'

'Are youse getting on the drink?'

'No,' I said truthfully.

'All right, sexy. You go party and have fun.'

'I miss you.'

'I miss *you*. There's something I need to tell you.'

In his mouth, something freighted and gliding happened to *you*. It became a soft exhalation, a sigh. It was a source of fascination to me, the paces he put his vowels through. I spent hours on the phone, making him repeat certain words. Say *pussy* again. 'Puss-eh.' Say *work* again. 'Werrrk.' Say *fire* again. 'Fi-yah.' Say *sure* again. 'Shower.'

'Go on, then.'

'I lost nine hundred quid last night. On the roulette.'

I placed my forehead against the window. A seagull was floating outside, held aloft on eddying thermals. Briefly, our eyes met through the glass. It gave a cry and wheeled away.

'Oh, well done,' I said.

*

Si-*eed*. He had a beautiful, broad-boned face, like a racially indeterminate video girl. Although he wasn't racially indeterminate, not to me. I knew his ethnicity (English/Malay). I knew how many brothers he had (he was the youngest of four). I knew the genesis of his parents' relationship (illicit). I knew where he was born (Orkney, where his father once worked as a short-order chef). I knew where he'd idled away teenage weekends (Bradford Ice Arena). I knew the name of the Algerian rig he'd worked on before moving here (T-211, on the edge of Reggane District, in Adrar Province). I knew how he'd felt when he was flown over the Sahara in one of those tinny little charter planes, 'like the one Aaliyah died in' (scared). I knew more about him than I did about some of my friends, though we'd met only three times before today.

Our first date was an afternoon debrief over coffee, to check we had two heads between us. I was still missing some kitchen utensils, so asked him to come to Marks and Spencer with me to buy a tin opener. He picked up the first one he saw – an over-priced, brushed steel number – and I was forced to buy it, since I didn't want to look cheap. The thing was sitting in my dish rack now, gleaming insolently, as if aware of its inflated price tag and the fraudulent process that bought it immunity.

He met me on the corner of my street. He was taking me to a festival in a fairground, to meet his back to back and their friends. It struck me as a bizarre agenda. Festivals should be in fields, and meeting friends was something proper couples did. But what did I know? I was feeling my way, in this brave new era of accelerated contact.

He was unlike most of the men I'd spoken to. He was a grad-uate, being groomed for senior management. After Aberdeen, he was going to Brunei. After that, who knew? Maybe central Asia. There were Kazakh girls on his course at university. They were *unbelievable*. Literally so: they came with opaque agendas, unsay-able wants. Danger meant something different over there. He'd heard stories about villagers who used wolves as guard dogs, and

Caspian rigs with netting on the side and no choppers. Boats dropped workers at the foot of the platform, and they were left to scramble up onto the deck. Not that a modern rig guaranteed your safety. Look at the Macondo Incident. I'd probably know it as Deepwater Horizon, he added, though no driller called it that. Naming the disaster after the drill rig was a ploy by BP to divert the focus onto Transocean.

Parts of Kazakhstan were supposed to be beautiful, though that wasn't the first word that sprang to mind when he saw the bleak stretches of steppe along the coast. Rather, it seemed a place where nature and industry fought a war of attrition, with casualties on both sides. They said the Caspian might end up a desiccated moonscape, like the Aral. It was shrinking, and no one knew why. The north end of the sea was already shallow, and froze solid in winter. They built an archipelago to protect the rigs from ice, right through the migration path of the sturgeon. Fish stocks dropped, seals washed up dead on the shore. Nature avenged every one, by infusing the oil with so much sulphur the pipes cracked, and production shut down as soon as it began.

Kashagan was an elephant – a field of more than 500 million barrels – yet its reserves were inaccessible. The project had taken so long to complete it was already an anachronism, conceived when oil was a hundred dollars a barrel. It was worth half that now, and once a field the size of Kashagan went onstream, the price would only drop further. But what was the alternative? They could hardly leave it to rot.

On the dock road, a freezing wind blew in off the sea, whipping the oily water into white tipped curls and crests. I pulled my coat around me, and remarked he must be feeling the cold since Algeria. He shook his head. Algeria was colder than you'd think. He was there in December and had to sleep in a tracksuit, with a hoodie over the top. More than anything, it reminded him of the

post-apocalyptic films of his boyhood: *Mad Max, Resident Evil.*
Burned-out cars, a few flares in the distance, sand running out to
the horizon, as flat and featureless as the sea itself. There, the
storms that grounded flights and shut down operations were
sandstorms: billowing, velvety cliffs of dust, with the same luxurious look as well fires. The sky turned yellow, the sun glowed
red. It was like a reckoning at the ends of the earth.

In some respects, T-211 was more isolated than a platform on
the far side of the Shetland Basin. There was no internet, no
reception. He had to trudge out into the dunes and hold his
phone above his head to get a signal. The plant was built for work
and sleep and nothing else. The crew only had a few phrases of
English, and his Arabic wasn't up to much.

On that first hitch, expecting something like the floating hotels
of the North Sea, he didn't even bring a book. The rig's sole
amenity was a running track, which circled the compound and
ran right out into the desert. Some nights he'd go out and turn a
few morose circuits, but mostly he sat in his room and stared at
the walls, allowing his boredom to curdle until he was so lethargic
he could barely move. He ought to have been there now, except
someone told the authorities he was only twenty-five, so he was
expelled from the country, along with his back to back. They were
currently cooling their heels in a Rose Street flat.

'My friend was married to an Algerian man,' I said. 'Well, half
Algerian. He was actually from Lewisham. He was an arsehole.
She's divorcing him now.'

He looked at me sideways. His eyes were a murky, occidental
green. *True story*, I almost said. I was yelling from the other side
of the generational divide. His friends had not yet started marry-
ing. Mine were already getting divorced. Sometimes, when I
thought of all the things my contemporaries had accrued in the
years I spent with Adam, I felt a sick lurch, as when you suddenly

realise you've forgotten something important, something crucial. And I *had* forgotten something crucial – that women do not get an infinite number of chances to remake their lives. I took an unhealthy interest in my friends' divorces (the opposite side of the coin to my wedding-induced *ennui*). I used to think this was because couples always got married for the same reason, whereas when they got divorced, it was for reasons all their own. Though lately, I'd started noticing my divorced friends' stories were similar, once the details were stripped back.

'I'll never understand this,' said Said. 'Why do women marry arseholes?'

I gnawed at my thumbnail. My nails were painted with clear varnish, spiked with chips of red. An adult expression of a childhood preference. As a little girl, I'd loved all things translucent: jelly shoes inlaid with glitter; Perspex bags overlaid with painted bows; ball pens with liquid-filled barrels, inset with drifting underwater seascapes or volleys of floating hearts. The varnish splintered under my tooth.

'Lassitude? Not wanting to go back to the start? If you're with someone that long, you want *something* to show for it.'

'Sunk cost fallacy.'

'What?'

'Sunk cost fallacy. We did it in economics. If you walk to the shop, then remember it's closed because it's a Sunday, you don't carry on walking because you've got halfway, do you? But people carry on throwing good money after bad, even when it's clear a project won't bear fruit.'

'If I'd known there was a name for that, my life would be so different.'

He was less handsome when he smiled. It disrupted the perfect oval of his face.

'There you go. Every day's a school day.'

We turned onto the esplanade. The tide was out. The sea was a smudged line in the distance. The ghostly outline of a tanker was just visible, a half-tone darker than the sky.

'What about you?' he said, one émigré to another. 'Do you miss London?'

'Not really,' I said.

I offered an abridged version of events. The burglary; the book. I missed out the tax rebate, the twin revelations. We crossed the road and walked towards the fairground. The Ferris wheel churned against a bank of thickening cloud. Children swarmed around us, weaving through the gaudy forest of fake palms. They fed coins into banks of chirruping slot machines and crowded around the grabbers, sticky palms pressed flat against the glass, like inmates in a prison's visitation booth. The toilets were at the back of the bowling alley, and a long queue of adults with rattling jaws and vast pupils lined up alongside the ninth birthday parties and tentatively flirting teenagers.

'Why are there so many children?' I said.

'To be fair, we're on their turf. Not the other way round.'

The sullen thump of house was faintly audible over the screams from the waltzers. We found Said's friends in a cordoned-off section behind the log flume. His back to back, a wily, fox-faced boy who barely looked older than the teenage patrons of the arcade, told us he'd been chatting up a blonde at the bar, and she interrupted him to say they'd met the week before at Tunnels, and he'd used all the same lines then. Aberdeen was small; there were too few women to go around.

In a dark corner of the marquee, Said tapped a small heap of dun crystals into my hand. I licked my palm, and winced. That taste. I'd never got used to it. I gestured for his drink. He nodded dolorously.

'Should have bombed it.'

I looked around. Everyone was so young. They were all wearing Air Max and doing that funny little shuffle people used to do at Bowlers. Done right, it looks effortless, as if you're being borne backwards on a travelator. The music sounded old too. I listened as it resolved itself into something recognisable. Lennie De Ice: 'We Are I.E.' Voodoo. A dark and irresistible command to dance. I could still remember the first time I heard it out, at a cavernous Birmingham club that was once a church. Back then, we were hurtling towards the new millennium, moving so fast music more than four years old was classed as 'old school'. They were sad songs, under the hectic breakbeats. The 'happy' appellation came later. Their rinky-dink vocals sounded distant, unreachable, like a carnival rolling out of town. Or maybe that was my experience of hardcore, colouring my perception. We had arrived late, late to the party. By the time we got there, most people had packed up and gone.

'Look at that,' I said to Said, tugging on his arm and pointing upwards.

There was a gap between the marquee's walls and its roof. Through it, the rollercoaster was visible. As he looked, a clattering car of children appeared above the canvas ridge, like a folly glimpsed through a gap in a hedge. They sat poised at the prow of the track for a moment, their faces white and solemn, as the gears cranked and turned beneath them. Then they swept down, and disappeared from view.

*

'You're very vulpine, aren't you?' I said. 'Do people tell you that all the time?'

'No they fucking don't, because I don't work with people like you, who use nice words like *vulpine*.'

Said's back to back grinned sourly. I took his cheeks between my fingers and squeezed, as if testing the give of a peach.

'You're very vulpine, and very clever. You remind me of Mr Tod. Do you move house every time you get in a mood?'

'I don't think I'm that clever. It's more … I'm quite open-minded, like.'

'Are you, yeah? Fit for a Californian encounter group?'

'I don't mean that. What I'm trying to say is …'

His brow was creased with the effort of trying to think. He frowned down at the lit end of his cigarette.

'Ah, fuck it. I don't know what I'm trying to say.'

I took the cigarette from between his lips. If there is a greater pleasure than smoking on pills (the tobacco tastes sweet, sweeter than usual; each draught produces a small, ancillary rush) I have yet to find it. Music drifted out from the tent, distorted by distance. The urge to dance nagged at me, like a toddler tugging at its mother's skirts. I made a few minimal movements with my feet. The problem with music these days was … what *was* the problem? My mind was making long synaptic stretches and I kept losing my train of thought. Ah. That was it. The problem with music these days was that it had gone good again. Music had gone good again, drugs had gone good again, so the temptation to go out and get on it, for the jobless person, on leave from adult life, was always there.

I had a rule about taking pills (once a year, in Ibiza), but I'd relaxed it since moving here. I was on sabbatical, and could do as I liked. There was a latitude that came with looking young. Or younger than the indigenous population, at least. *What do you call a pretty girl in Scotland? A tourist.* In Aberdeen, the old joke was no laughing matter. Never had I seen such a high concentration of homely people all packed into one place. The men on Tinder who claimed to be thirty looked nearer to fifty. The strippers were

Polish, the prostitutes Romanian, a situation that said as much about their host city's limitations as their home region's economic straits.

My letting agent was a liar, by the way. They were still there, sulkily plying their trade at the end of the street. Sometimes I saw them on the dock road, holding terse negotiations with men outside pubs. They dressed for the weather, in parkas and jeans, but you could spot them by their high-contrast colouring. They had bleached blonde hair, the silvery shade of an MGM starlet's, but their skin was brown, and their eyes were so dark it was hard to tell the iris from the pupil.

'This is my brother,' I said to the man next to us, gesturing to the back to back. 'Do you think we look alike?'

'I can see a certain resemblance,' he said. 'You've got the same nose. He's better looking than you, though.'

'Our mother thinks so too,' I tipped my head back and exhaled. 'This one's her favourite. He's spoilt by all the women in our family. He's the only boy *and* he's the baby, by a long margin. You were a happy little accident, weren't you, squelcher? Everyone thought he was going to have three heads.'

I squeezed his cheeks again. He took a step back, his expression wounded.

'Maw never told me that!'

'Look at the *age* gap sometime. Surely you didn't think you were planned? Thought you were meant to be the clever one?'

I turned to the man.

'They *paid* for his education, you know. My sister and I had to make do with the local comp, but he went to Glenalmond. They wanted to send him to Gordonstoun, but they thought the cold showers might make him cry.'

The man narrowed his eyes, possibly against the cloud of smoke I'd blown in his direction.

'If you two are brother and sister, how come you've got an English accent and he doesn't?'

'That's a good question ... I left Glasgow to go to university and never went back. I lived in London, then Johannesburg, and I had to flatten my accent out there, because no one could understand me. Also, women lose and pick up accents quicker than men. Like sponges. Because we're more adaptable, more eager to please.'

With the inclusion of fact, my lie felt more convincing. It tripped off my tongue as fluently as the truth.

'That sounds like pish,' the back to back muttered.

'It's not *pish*. They've done studies and things. Split your pill with me, will you? I know you've got one left.'

'Get to fuck.'

He grinned, just like a real brother, taking pleasure in refusal. He was flickering in front of me. I blinked twice, to reset my vision. He had one of those amazing faces that looked to be balanced on higher struts than most. His teeth slanted inwards. His eyes were the impenetrable black of a bull shark's.

'I love how you *respected* that decision, by the way,' he said.

'I didn't respect it. You're being tight. But then, you never did learn to share.'

I turned back to the man.

'Isn't my brother horrid? Isn't he selfish? This is what comes of being a *de facto* only child.'

He considered us for a minute.

'This boy's really your brother? He looks about ten.'

'We kept him in a sealed crate for most of his childhood. That's why he's got such nice skin. No sun damage.'

'Have you got a boyfriend?' the man said abruptly.

'Kind of,' I replied.

I was still stunned by the week's revelations. I should have been in glory, but what I felt was closer to the tranced horror of a child who has struck a match and somehow set fire to the curtains. It scared me that Caden was prepared to do this, with only minimal prompting. It should have been harder; everyone told me it would be harder. *Married men never leave their wives.* And yet, I always knew he would. I had a sense that if I led by example, if I left my job and the city where I lived, if I showed him how easy it was to simply walk away from things, he would follow. I was shocked and unsurprised, at the same time.

Perhaps what I felt belonged to that nameless order of emotions we all feel before we learn to talk, and make binary distinctions. Language has these glitches. *Right.* The word we use to describe a chemical spell strong enough to scramble the moral compass, a blood cypher unlocked by scent and facial symmetry, also means 'correct'. No one else would think it right. The law would protect her, and when the time came, weigh her contribution to their marriage and give her money in exchange for love, as if the two were interchangeable. And when we lived together, we would lie about how we met, and when, and this deception would implicate us, would suggest that somewhere, buried beneath our brazen new happiness, the ineluctable rightness of our love, was the knowledge we'd done something very wrong.

'Where is he, then?' said the man. 'This kind-of boyfriend?'

'Offshore,' I said. 'He's coming home next week.'

The back to back sighed, and flicked his cigarette over a low perimeter wall. It whirled through the air, shedding sparks, and landed on the damp concrete beyond with a hiss. I'd always envied people who could do this. It belonged to the same suite of skills as whistling with two fingers and cutting a deck of cards; deft and worldly capabilities I classed as male, without knowing why.

He took my hand and led me back across the astroturf. His grip was loose and incidental, his touch surprisingly warm.

'Is that a onesie?' he said, over his shoulder.

'It's a *jumpsuit*.'

'Same thing, but.'

'I'm more or less constantly in a jumpsuit,' I boasted into thin air. 'I've got this dress, the slut dress, I was going to wear that, but my legs are covered in bruises, because I keep walking into my bed. I love a jumpsuit. They make me feel like Betty Catroux at Studio 54. When in doubt, wear a jumpsuit. That's what I always say.'

He stopped, and leant against the marquee. His eyes were closing. He had the pretty, lilac lids of the pale-skinned. He passed a hand over his face.

'Jesus Christ, I am absolutely fucking *fried*,' he said. 'What were you saying just now?'

Though it was he leaning on the tent, and not me, I could feel the canvas against his neck, the breath of wind, lifting the hairs on his scalp. My skin tingled in response. This used to happen sometimes when I was younger: a vault of perception so keen, it was like being psychic.

'Doesn't matter,' I said.

We struggled to find Said. The space had filled up while we were gone and he was small. I kept tripping over my own feet and knocking into people.

'Where have you *been*?' he said, when we finally found him. He was where we left him, more or less: the pivot around which the night swung.

'I don't *know*,' I yelled into his ear. 'We got waylaid. We were smoking outside with this lad who seemed really stupid.'

'Naw, naw,' the back to back said hotly. 'He wasnae stupid. He was sound. He said I was better looking than her.'

'Well he was *wrong*,' I shouted. My voice sounded hoarse and high-toned in my ears. 'He was only saying that because he knew you were dead open-minded.'

'Come and dance,' said Said. 'You were saying the other day you never got the chance to any more. Now you keep running off.'

It was a coincidence too neat for fiction, I thought, as we pushed our way through bodies, that these boys were so different. They felt symbolic: the platonic ideal of a driller and his back to back. Two friends functioning at opposite ends of a continuum; two halves of a single mechanism, oscillating busily. Said was dark, the back to back fair. Said was constant, the back to back changeable. Said was soft featured, the back to back all angles. Said used language economically, the back to back was a talker, tossing out rapid sentences that sounded like machine-gun fire. I fell somewhere in the middle; halfway between the back to back's pinging mercury and Said's solid, earthbound presence.

We found space near the front, and the back to back spun off ahead. From time to time, we'd see him some way in front of us, zipping about, pointy nose held high in the air, like Mr Rush. More than once, I turned Said's wrist and looked at his watch, but the numbers melted and reconfigured before my eyes. I could feel the tick of his pulse beneath my fingers. It was somehow connected to my blood, and the collective bounce around us. He came from Bradford, that hot, dark forge that once shook a nation: bleeps and bass, portentous sub-low frequencies. I thought of this, and a smile sprang to my lips.

'I'm glad I met you,' I said.

'What?'

'I *said*: I'm glad I met you.'

He smiled so vaguely, I thought he hadn't heard. Then he folded me into his arms and hugged me. A hug so warm and meant, it leached into my soul. It is still in there somewhere, I think.

'I'm glad I met you too.'

My mind was uncoiling now, on a languorous backwards loop. I thought about hooliganism, how our idiom ended up strewn with brutal metaphors (we nailed lem, battered tablets, caned drugs), how that was down to their uneasy late-eighties armistice. 'World in Motion'. Wasn't that about the *entente*? A brief and beautiful moment in time when it felt like we had it all to play for. I thought about dancing, how I still danced a bit like a boy, which was a legacy of my adolescence, when I went to clubs with my boyfriend and his friends and learned to dance by watching them. My generation had been the last batch of girls who danced *properly*, which is to say they wore trainers and made no attempt to look sexy. I never thought there was a genetic component to dancing, until I met up with my sister in Ibiza one year, and discovered that she and I, dancing under the sullen Spanish sun, moved in exactly the same way (a pensive little two-step I always thought of as 'the bear dance').

And Caden. All night, he'd been swimming up through my thoughts like a fish, though I tried to push him back down. Every time I remembered the enormity of what he was about to do, the share of responsibility I'd have to bear, my stomach seized. Ordinary nerves; a squirm of paranoia. This was it. We were together and would have to remain so, for the rest of our lives. I could never leave him. I couldn't allow him to dismantle his marriage, abandon his family, then dump him ten minutes later because I'd met someone I preferred; because his wife was a nuisance and his children were awful; because the difference between *too* and *to* continued to elude him, and every time he confused them, it made me gnash my teeth. We were going to do so much damage. We were running up a debt we'd never settle.

But already, I was struggling to imagine a future without him. He was mine, he was mine. He belonged to me. I knew he might still change his mind again, break my heart, fracture his own. And when I thought of that, when I thought of my own heart being broken, I was clutched by a larger fear. I had to help him. If I didn't help him, he would drown. And if he drowned, he'd be lost to me for good.

Abruptly, the set changed gear. The music turned tougher, more imperative. Out of the wordless textures, a voice emerged, heard over a thin ripple of applause:

You know, sometimes we're not prepared for adversity.

The words, their firm exactitude, pricked my consciousness, and produced a tingling sensation all over my skin. The message was there, embedded in the music: Come forward. Get it done. The track dropped out for a second, and the room rushed in to the fill the vacuum, whooping, clapping, whistling. I liked it when people clapped in clubs. It was irrelevantly civilised behaviour, like when football fans gave former players standing ovations their first time back at the old ground. And it was true what they said about northern crowds. Even this far north, in a staid and venal town that only cared for oil.

I wondered where the back to back had gone, and as I did, he reappeared. I reached up and hugged him. He was so little. His body was like a fine silken thread in my arms. He put two fingers in his mouth and blew. The sound, when it came, trilled like a car alarm. I smiled to myself, an inward wager settled.

★

'Did you know that people from Glasgow and Liverpool have a natural affinity? It's the Irish in them. That's why they talk quickly and take a lot of drugs. Big, poor, wet cities. The west coast trifecta. It produces a certain personality type.'

I was addressing the back to back as he tacked a wayward course in front of Said and me, stepping off the kerb, then onto it, then off it, then onto it again. His T-shirt was too big (at least, it looked too big, to my thirty-something eye) and kept slipping off one shoulder. He looked like the last up.

'I'll say this for you,' said the back to back. 'You can handle a fucking pill.'

'I should think *so*,' I replied, with a hint of old-maid asperity. 'I've been taking them twenty years.'

'So you took your first tablet when I was two.'

'Let's not dwell on the numbers too much.'

'I reckon I can get on with anyone, really.'

'Is that because you're dead open-minded?'

'Ah man, you can tell you're a journalist. You get the one angle, and *exploit* it, relentlessly. You're like the British media in human form. You're like the fucking *Sun*.'

'I'm not a journalist. Not any more.'

'What are you, then?' said Said.

'I don't know,' I said. 'A writer without portfolio, I suppose.'

Over the docks, the sky was streaked with pink. To summer in Aberdeen is to know how near the Arctic Circle is. The evenings are relentlessly bright; the dawn chorus starts at three. It was worse, they said, on the northerly rigs: the Eider, the Cormorant, the Tern. Three hundred miles north, June meant white nights and countervailing sunlight. A crazy-making subversion of diurnal rhythms. It was worse than winter even, when the sea reared up and hurled itself against the legs of the rig as if the two were engaged in a blood feud. Northerners have no fear of the dark. They're inured to it, to a certain extent.

We walked to a casino at the west end of town. The building had a cinderblock ceiling and a drab, municipal look. A place you'd go to address your need to gamble, not indulge it. We don't do casinos well in this country; they run counter to the principles that made our nation great. Of course Aberdeen, a city that abhorred spending, a city grown fat on thrift, would make a particularly poor fist of it. Inside, the air was stale. The clockless walls were covered with flock paper.

Said went to the bar. The back to back drifted over to the roulette wheel, where he started a conversation with a man in a lightweight pink suit. The man had a prematurely reddened face, and wore the sleeves of his jacket pushed back, *Miami Vice* style. He suited being here, with his bookmaker's clothes and his seedy aspect. They stopped talking as I walked up.

'What are you saying to my brother?' I said. 'Anything you say to him, you have to run by me first.'

'This boy's no your brother,' the man scoffed. 'I was at college with him.'

Over the course of the night, I had become attached to my lie. I was used to being someone's big sister, I suppose.

'He doesn't like to talk about me, because I'm older. We're not in the same peer group.'

'I was asking if he'd heard George FitzGerald's album.'

'Who's George FitzGerald?'

It sounded like a band leader's name.

'Are you joking?'

'No.'

'You've just been to see him.'

I shrugged. Paying attention to specifics was what teenage boys did. I'd no sooner choose to go to a club because of the lineup than I would plaster my bedroom wall with flyers for Dreamscape and Pandemonium. Talk around us resumed. 'That album's about his bird,' said someone. 'What *time* is it?' said someone else.

'It all sounds the same to me now,' I said. 'Like nineties garage, which you're probably too young to remember. Producers now are such ... copies. Bicep – they're copies. Their version of that Dominica song, it's just the original song! I know, because I've got it, on a Stu Allan tape, from 1995. It's no different.'

I spent the first decade of the new millennium complaining that music wasn't as good as it used to be, the last few years alarmed by the rate at which my past was being pillaged. Hearing it, I felt a kind of vertigo, as if the twenty years between had been annulled. As if no time had passed at all. Garage mainlined everything good that had gone before (the frictionless gloss of house; the sadness and longing of early hardcore) and somehow made it *more*. It sounded like a hole in the heart, like the incommunicable ache that comes with a life spent looking backwards. It never gained traction in the north-west. Liverpool was too white, too wedded to the four/four signature.

'I love old garage.'

Said had materialised at the table, with drinks.

'I know you do, baby,' I said. 'That's because you have taste.'

I tucked an arm round his shoulder.

'That's how I knew we'd be friends. I knew both of you would be my friends as soon as we met. I've got this thing with my best mate, we call it our friendship butterfly net, and when we meet someone we like ...'

'Yes, yes,' said the back to back. 'We've heard plenty about the butterfly net already.'

My face hurt. I suffered from bruxism, silent lament of the stressed. I'd not helped my case by grinding my teeth and talking rubbish all night. I flexed my jaw. The back to back patted his pockets down and handed me some gum.

'Your little friend looks unsavoury,' I said, chewing.

'He *is* unsavoury,' said the back to back. 'That's the word.'

'I don't think you should talk to him any more. I don't think you should be squandering the family silver on a game of chance. Why not count some cards?'

'Away to fuck! I'm no in any state to card count. I can barely see the table as it is.'

He pushed his chips onto the baize with a sweeping gesture. The croupier called to us, and as he did, everyone took a single step back and turned to watch the wheel. The ball shuttled around in its gulley. My pill had burned down, leaving in its place a ticking contentment, but as I stepped back it gave a vestigial kick, so that my vision skipped a few frames, and the table leered up at me, its white numbers arcane and coded like Ouija script, its cloth an unreal green. They say François Blanc cut a deal with the devil to obtain the secrets of the game. What secrets are there? Everyone knows which way the odds are stacked.

I still had my arm around Said's shoulder, and I felt him brace beside me, as though it was his money on the table, not his friend's. The ball clattered through its final revolution and settled in the bracket with a click. The back to back turned round and smiled so winningly, it took me a second to understand he had lost. He put a hand over his mouth, like a pinup girl pantomiming shock, then extended it towards us. A pill, split three ways, lay on his palm.

We place our bets and we gamble. We imagine we have what it takes to beat the house.

I was in the pub one night and this woman went to sit down next to me, so I moved my coat out of the way. She laughed at me, because the coat was pink. I said, 'It's not pink. It's light plum.' Bit of banter, you see? Broke the ice. I fuck her the way I can't fuck my wife. Throw her about the room. Bit of strangulation. It's different, more animalistic. I've only seen her a couple of times, but when I'm offshore, I talk to her more than I talk to my missus. I don't know if I miss her, but I miss the things she says to me. She tells me I look strong. My wife doesn't say those things. And I don't want to say 'Look, I need to hear this' and then for her to go 'Oh, you look nice' straight away, all robotic and that. But I do need to hear it. Massively. Turning thirty hurt me. My hair started falling out.

FIVE

TERN

'How did you get that scar?'

'You don't *ask* people that. You can't just sit down and start asking questions like that. Do you not know anything? It's a little bit personal, that.'

It wasn't the Welsh boy who spoke, but the man sitting opposite me. He had the light, affectless stare of a serial killer, but his tone was chiding, school-teacherly. Faced with him, I felt as I did when I was at school: sullen, resistant to correction.

'I'm interviewing him,' I said. 'I have to ask questions.'

The scar was a deep, curving crevice that ran all the way down his face, from his eyelid to the corner of his mouth. The skin had an unhealthy purple tint to it, the yellowed lilac of a fading bruise. Unthinkingly, he passed a hand over his cheek. His eyes slipped past my shoulder as his focus settled somewhere else, somewhere interior.

'Warring,' he said.

'Don't tell lies.'

He grinned.

'Fell off a log when I was six.'

'Onto what? A scythe?'

'We're not *that* country. The log was at the edge of a quarry. I rolled right down.'

It was half past one on a Tuesday afternoon, and I was already on my way to being drunk. I'd been circulating around this room for a few hours now, buying drinks, inviting confidences, like the tipsy hostess of a dour, exclusively male cocktail party. These three men, I thought, could be ranked in order of hostility. The first found my presence an imposition, and wished I would go. His friend, who had just come back from the bar with four Southern Comforts and lemonade, apparently taking the Welsh boy at his word when he told him to 'get anything', didn't care either way. And the Welsh boy, who was, as far as I could tell, the dominant force at the table, wanted me to stay.

The nature of this work was making me see what it must be like for them. Going up to groups, identifying the most receptive, inveigling your way in, uncaring of what the majority wants. Girls are taught to respond to the subtlest social cues, to beat a retreat at the first hint of furrowed brow or crossed arms; boys to develop a benign tone deafness for the very same signals. They learn to brazen it out and keep talking, like a salesman on a doorstep, sensing a soft no. In order to do work like this – to latch onto strangers and coax conversation from them – I had to become a hybrid of sorts. The unthreatening looks of a woman. The impervious core of a man.

'What's your name, darling?' the Welsh boy said. He had a lilting Valleys accent, at the opposite end of the chromatic scale from the singing Teesside inflections around us.

'Dunyazad.'

'*Shut* the front door. Nobody's called that!'

'I am.'

'Fuck *me*. I ain't never met a Dunyazad before. I ain't never heard a name like that my whole life.'

'Well. Now you have.'

'You got a pen? Write your name down for me. Your *full* name. I don't want to miss this book when it comes out.'

'Put it in your phone.'

He looked at me as if I'd suggested inscribing it on his forehead.

'Can't do that. My missus goes through my phone, doesn't she?'

'In London, it is considered unacceptable to go through your partner's phone.'

'Well in Port Talbot, it's fine. I've got to keep my Facebook secret even.'

'You have a secret Facebook account?'

'I like nosing at people's photos. I hate the drama that goes with it.'

'I've noticed men who claim to "hate drama" are often quite good at causing it.'

'So birds in London aren't bothered about cheating?'

'It's not that they're not bothered. They are, but they cover it up, because they want to seem French. It's a bit tacky, to monitor your partner's movements. Like ... having a party after a christening.'

I pulled a lidless biro from the detritus at the bottom of my bag, tore a page from my notebook, and wrote *Dunyazad Jones* in a clear, round hand. He took the paper from me, held it up to the light and squinted at it, like a cashier checking a fifty.

'Tell you what, Dunyazad. They're some cracking boots you got on.'

The boots were lovely, in fact. They were dark blue, and finished at mid calf with a soft suede leg that folded back over the heels, like gaiters. A relic from my old life, where beauty was obtainable, and everything, but everything, was up for barter.

'I call them my horse leg boots. Because they make me look like a shire horse.'

'Neigh, they don't!' He glanced at them again. 'They're very nice, actually. Like fake Uggs.'

'They're Chloé.'

'Kind of collapsed in on themselves, aren't they? Cluggs!'

'I don't know why I bother wearing anything nice up here.'

'Aren't you supposed to be asking us about offshore?'

'So I am. Where do you work?'

'Not telling.'

'I bet I can guess. Let me see. You flew here direct, and you've not gone three and three yet. I reckon that puts you on ...' I tapped my mouth with my pen and narrowed my eyes. 'One of the *Brents*?'

The Welsh boy smirked.

'That's classified.'

'I'm going to say you work on the Tern. Same region, same weather.'

'Say Tern again.'

'Tern.'

'*Turn*. Quite posh, aren't you?'

'Not especially.'

'It's good, I like it. I like posh girls.'

'What's it like?'

He looked at me evenly. His eyes were the colour of honey. His hair and his eyes and his skin were all the same shade, which made it difficult to pick out his features, or form an organising impression of his face.

'It's all right,' he said.

'It's shite,' muttered the first man.

'It's what you *make* of it. See, I never bring my problems to work. Some people do. They're the ones who end up counting the days down till they go home. If you don't cut it off, it pickles your head. There was a man not long ago who filled his pockets with wrenches and threw himself off his rig.'

'I feel like I've heard that one before.'

'Maybe. The point remains. You *cannot* live one life, if you work offshore. You must live two.'

'You don't mind being away?'

'I have to be honest with you, my love, I don't. I'm a little bit cold-hearted like that.'

'I don't do Facebook, it drives me mad. You see people out there, doing their own heads in, thinking: "The missus is out again, doing this or doing that, and I'm stuck on here".'

It was the second man speaking, the one who had fetched the drinks. I was distracted by the incipient tension between the Welsh boy and his friend, and had almost forgotten he was there. I looked at him properly for the first time. He had a scaff's build – tall, with huge, rounded shoulders – and an anxious, florid face. There was a large tattoo of a football crest on his arm, partially obscured by the sleeve of his T-shirt, but what was visible, just below, was the phrase *Keep It Casual*, written in a jaunty, slanting font.

'A lot of the Boro lads are never off the phone, arguing with their birds. It's constant drama. Always drama.'

'Someone told me about a boy on the Beatrice,' I said. 'He headbutted his iPad because his girlfriend was going out and he couldn't stop her.'

'It's hard,' the second man said. 'I've got a missus and sprogs at home. My youngest has just turned one. She had a bit of a cough and she's been crying a lot in the night. The other night, my wife sent me three recordings of her screaming. I said: "Why the fuck have you sent me this?" She said: "Because I'm putting up with it, every single night".'

'What can you do about that, while you're away?'

'It's a bit of a cycle. She's at home, doing everything on her own. If she's in a foul mood when I ring, then we'll have a few days where we don't speak or we're arguing. Then you're bickering with everyone at work, because your head's up your arse. Then you make up, say you're sorry. We normally do two or three rounds each trip.'

He looked so downcast, I felt I ought to change the subject, but could think of nothing to say in that moment that didn't relate to marriage.

'You know, it's very common to fight with your wife when you work away. It's so common they have a name for it: Intermittent Husband Syndrome.'

'Is that a real thing?'

'It is. Soldiers get it too.'

These men were like soldiers, I thought. They had to cultivate a capacity to detach. They were in the business of maintaining civilisation. This work sent them out into the world's roughest wildernesses, and had a paradoxically coarsening effect on their behaviour. They liked to talk about hardship posts, to one-up each other with awful conditions. In Angola, they were hustled into a fleet of blacked-out SUVs and made to lie on the floor until they reached the heliport. In Nigeria, rigs came with bunkers shaped like upright coffins. If pirates seized control of the platform they were supposed to lock themselves in the bunkers and face Mecca. You could earn good money in Africa, but it was danger money.

So maybe they were more like mercenaries. Certainly, rigs were like barracks: all-male domains where anti-female paranoia flourished. Offshore, they swapped stories of grasping wives and scheming girlfriends, of women who 'trapped' them with pregnancies, spirited children away over borders, who pauperised them in divorce settlements, cheated on them with their friends. *Don't worry about your missus,* they'd say to each other. *She's not worrying about you. She's busy getting nailed by Leroy.*

Leroy is to oil workers as Jody is to Marines. A folk figure; the indolent civilian who hangs about on dry land, taking advantage of their absence. An expression of generalised anxiety, a means of hardening the heart towards home. Notably (or not) Leroy, like Jody, appears to be black, though most North Sea workers come from post-industrial towns that are, for the most part, white. Leroy, one man said, was name-checked all over the world. He'd worked in Brazil, Greenland, the US, the Falklands. Wherever he went, the men made jokes about Leroy. Why is he black? I asked the man. Why do you *think*? he replied.

'You've got your rig head and your home head,' the Welsh boy said. 'You have to communicate in different ways. Offshore, you speak abruptly. You can't leave any room for error. You can't skirt round issues. When you get off, you need a decompression period. People at home don't understand. Their reality goes on day to day. We're taken out of it for a while.'

The sun threw a pale quadrant across the car park. Something about this room, the angle at which the light hit the window, made it seem smoky, though smokers were corralled in the concrete yard outside. The air looked tinted, as if seen through tobacco-coloured glass. On the table in front of me, my phone lit up.

I'm here. Where are u???

'Going so soon?' the Welsh boy said, as I got up from my seat.

'I've got to go and get my boyfriend.'

'Let him wait.'

The first man shook his head, as if alive to me and my suite of sneaky tricks.

'*Boyfriend*. You must think we're soft. I've seen you going up to lads all day. I think you're a whore.'

'Shut up,' I said, picking up my bag. 'Nobody cares what you think.'

Caden was standing in roughly the same spot I'd first found him. Now, as then, he was listing under the weight of his kit bag. I loitered by the cashpoint for a minute, watching him. I had rehearsed this scene in my mind many times. I had seen myself standing at arrivals, grave and erect in spaghetti-strapped black (my outfit planned to evoke Kim Kardashian, courtside with Kanye, in the salad days of their romance; taupe lip liner, loose bun, look of candid love). I would put my arms around his neck and hold him, in silent recognition of his sacrifice. My mood should be muted, to match his. It would be *unseemly* to act too pleased. I assumed he'd feel a degree of ambivalence, so was prepared for a range of reactions: guilt, sadness, some light sulking. But I was not prepared for this.

As I approached, he looked up and grinned, so the brackets around his mouth disappeared, and a corresponding series of lines sprang around his eyes. He looked as happy as I'd ever seen him. His brows were raised, as if he couldn't quite believe his own daring. He had done it. He had orchestrated the heist of himself, and somehow pulled it off.

He held out his hands. 'Look!'

I looked down. He had beautiful hands, unexpectedly slim and attenuated, with slender fingers and oval nails. The hands of a taller man, with a nicer job.

'What am I looking at?'

'*Look!*'

I stared stupidly. His hands trembled. His body ran at a slightly higher frequency than most, and it was hard to tell whether these tremors were nerves or just a surfeit of unused energy. For a moment, I thought this was what he wanted to show me: that he was in such a state of extremity, his hands were shaking. And then I realised. No ring.

'Does it feel weird?'

He shrugged and smiled, together.

'Nah. I can't wear it at work anyway. Just didn't bother putting it back on.'

We walked outside, to the taxi rank. He kept squeezing my hand and smiling at me. His lateral smile. I was reminded of that first day, the way he smiled at me whenever I looked in his direction. *What should I say? Whatever you like. See now, I won't want to swear.*

We passed a group of men, heading into the building. They watched as we walked past them, their faces alert and interested. I felt sure they could tell Caden was married, and not to me. My face, dimly reflected in the taxi's blacked-out windows, said it clearly enough. I was nobody's wife. Nobody's business but my own. Without warning, Caden pulled me back towards him and kissed me. As he did, I turned my head, so his lips glanced off my cheekbone and the mistimed kiss smacked against my ear. For a second, my hearing sang and whined. Above us, the sun was filtered through a fine grey haze. It was as if we stood in the ambit of a bomb blast.

*

'I wouldn't *dare* buy them.'

'No one's asking you to,' I said, turning the trainers over. They were lilac, with a floral patterned swoosh. 'Air Max Ones are a design classic. I had a pair like this when I was fifteen. I wore them the first time I went to Bowlers. With a denim Wonderbra and denim knickers. This was back when you *could* go to Bowlers in your underwear and be left alone. It really went downhill after they got a bar.'

Caden looked back at me, his face impassive. He didn't want to hear about me at fifteen, when Bowlers had no bar. He'd already looked through photos and pronounced me better now. I was greedy for his past, he was bored by mine. It was one of several small inequities I accepted without thinking about it any further. He picked up a pair of trainers exactly like the ones he was wearing. He meant to bin the ones he wore as soon as we got home. I stared when he said this. To me, they looked as clean and startlingly white as the day I first saw them.

'You bin your shoes when they get dirty? Like Floyd Mayweather?'

'They've got to be *white* white,' he said. 'Can't cope with stains, me.'

He loved to shop, to tour the bright, air-conditioned cube of Union Square or the cold, brutalist tunnel of the Trinity Centre, buying things he didn't need, or contemplating their purchase for another day. He had a zeal for accrual – the box fresh, the brand new, the untouched – but anticipating things he might buy in the near future gave him pleasure too. This was how he and Rachel filled their days when he was home. Staking out areas of acquisition. Shopping, spending, steadily consuming.

In John Lewis, he dismissed the racks of neat polo shirts and sports jackets (*It's got to be Ralph Lauren, Hugo Boss, or nothing*), but paused at a fifty-inch flat screen. He had been profoundly shocked to learn I didn't own a television. At home, he had eight: one in each bedroom, one in the lounge, one in the playroom, one in the conservatory and one in the bathroom. When I asked why he had a television in the bathroom, he looked at me as if I must be very stupid. Because sometimes, he explained, he wanted to watch television when he was in the bath.

In the Apple shop, he stopped in front of some expensive watches in a glass display case.

'Might try and bribe the twins,' he muttered.

Since this was said more to himself than me, it didn't require an answer. In the privacy of my head, I'd already drawn my own conclusions about the twins (obscenely, ruinously spoiled), his parenting (poor) and what would happen if I were put in charge (they would be bundled into a calèche and conveyed due south, like the young Jonathan Harker, until they reached AFC Harrogate). Maybe Rachel would stay so consumed with fury she'd never let me meet them. I crossed my fingers in my pocket, and counted the watches in the display case. Six: a number of bad omen. So she *would* allow a meeting, and before the year was out.

'What do you reckon?' he said, turning back to me.

'Maybe pull your horns in. For now.'

'But if I spend all my money now, there'll be nothing left for her to take.'

I traced an arabesque on the floor with my toe (straight for duty; curved for beauty). I still couldn't believe he'd signed a binding contract without checking what it might cost to dissolve, but I suppose, in this respect, he was no different from most.

'That isn't how divorce works,' I said.

We left the shop and wandered through town, tugged by some homing instinct back to Belmont Street. He stopped only once, to point out a corner where he was once picked up by police with some men from the Murchison.

'We were toy fighting. One of the lads picked me up then dropped me straight back down. I had bruises all over for weeks.'

Ova. In his mouth, it had the cheerful lilt of a Nordic greeting.

'Do you mean play fighting? Toy fighting sounds like you were arguing over dolls and bits of Meccano.'

'That's what it's called by ours.'

Some of his strangeness came back to me. There was a rural skew to his sentences, a country syntax I'd always attributed to his being born on the wrong side of the Pennines: *Straight to bed for me now,* he used to say. *That's me done for the night.*

'I think men use play fighting as a cover to get a real dig in.'

'None of *my* mates would do that.'

'What's the difference, when you end up with bruises either way?'

The conversation had taken us up to the bar we sat in that first night, when the snow settled onto the window frames and fell outside in deep, silent drifts. Only now the sun was out and the scent of resin rose off the timber slats of the terrace, merging with exhaust fumes from the bypass below. We sat in a glass-walled annexe that looked out over the treetops. The sun was filtered through the foliage, so the light took on a greenish tinge. On the terrace, a large Rottweiler was panting under a table. His eyes were mournful, his mollusc-dark gums dripped with saliva. He saw me looking, and looked back. His expression said he wanted me for a friend, that he wished the two of us could meet, today.

'We should get a rescue dog,' I said.

Caden shook his head. He was wearing mirrored sunglasses – another newly fashionable piece of nineties ephemera – so when I looked at him, I could see only myself, slightly warped by the curve of the lens.

'We're getting a puppy.'

'I want a rescue dog.'

'You don't know where it's been. It might have had a bad experience with its last owners. It might have been used for fighting.'

He ticked off contingencies on his fingers.

'You don't how old it is. It might be ill. Or impossible to train. It might bite the twins.'

The twins might bite *it*, I thought. Whenever he mentioned them, my Protestant grandma's maxim came to me: *Red hair, no bloody good*. The phrase danced hotly before my eyes, displacing any sensible response. I'd try and think of something banal to say about childhood, to pluck an encouraging story from my past (a juvenile delinquent turned surgeon; a wraith from the Ford now running a hedge fund) and come up with nothing. *Red hair, no bloody good*, my mind chanted. *Red hair, no bloody good*.

'I like the idea of taking in a dog that's had a rotten start in life. Spoiling it, giving it loads of love. Making up for all the stuff that's gone before.'

'I'm not arguing about it. We're getting a puppy.'

'The only reason you don't want a rescue dog is because you see it as a missed opportunity to waste loads of money.'

'We're not getting a second-hand dog.'

'And how would you like it if I said that about husbands?'

'That's different.'

'Do you know it's almost four months, to the day, that we came here?'

'Time flies.'

I reached out and fingered the cuff of his grey tracksuit.

'I like this. You look like all my borstal fantasies made flesh.'

'I wore it special.'

The annexe was filling up. The sun beat down on the glass panels, the air inside grew warm. The room was full of plants, like a greenhouse. The jungle breath of succulents hung heavy in the air. The girls around us were wearing shapes I remembered from my teens: crop tops, palazzo pants, slip dresses. Only this time, they paired them with stripes of mink contour that looked slightly muddy in the greenish light, and hair dyed confectionery colours. Lavender, light blue, rose gold, mint. The colours were beautiful once the eye adjusted to the artifice. Teetering on high heels, they reminded me of flowers on delicate stems, or the modern, etiolated versions of the chunky plastic ponies I collected as a child. It was like being in a hothouse, hemmed in by roses.

Caden took my hand and kissed it.

'Know what I love about being with you?'

'What?'

'It's like being on holiday. See, even when I go on holiday …'

He tailed off. Had it just hit him, that he was unlikely to ever go away with his children again? Or was he editing himself, out of tact? He didn't look like a man contemplating the full ruination of his family life. He was still smiling, so broadly it looked like it must hurt.

'It won't always be like this. We need to find somewhere to live.'

'I'll find us somewhere nice. I promise.'

'I'll need to find a job.'

'I don't want you worrying about all that. I make enough for both of us. I looked after Rachel. I'm going to look after you.'

'Did you ever think this would happen?'

'No. My mam did, though. She knew I wasn't happy with Rachel. She said she tried to convince herself I was, but deep down, she knew I wasn't.'

'Is she going to hate me?'

'She's going to *love* you. They all will.'

'Do you have a picture of her?'

He picked his phone up from the table and held it out for inspection.

'My mam. My nana. My Auntie Tessa. Auntie Karen. Auntie Val. Our Leanne. Our Madison. Our Courtney. Our Jade.'

A harem of relatives shuttled past, frozen in attitudes of female bonding: posing in bandage dresses outside pink-painted lavatory stalls, or lined up in someone's lounge, champagne glasses held aloft, toes pointed outwards, as if about to break into a Bob Fosse-style routine. His mother had his delicate, pointed chin and husky coloured eyes. Or rather, he had hers. She looked ludicrously young, a woman for whom the term *milf* might have been coined. I'd always imagined Stockton-on-Tees as a strictly female place, Aberdeen's inverse, with every man of marriageable age offshore. Looking at his pictures, it was easy to believe this was right.

'Are there no men in your family?'

'Only my dad. They're split up.'

'Do you still see him?'

'When he's about. He works away.'

Away. Locations in his stories were rarely specified. They were urban antimatter, defined solely in relation to Stockton-on-Tees, the town they were not.

'What's he like?'

'He's all right. His head's fell off a bit now. No one to keep him on the straight and narrow.'

'Does he miss your mum?'

'He'd have her back tomorrow.'

'Does she miss him?'

He laughed. He had a surprisingly deep, carrying laugh. It was deeper than his voice, which barely travelled beyond his sphere of personal space.

'Nah! She hung on till I was sixteen. And then ...'

'Hit her pain threshold?'

'She says she wishes she left the first time she thought of it.'

Sixteen was the age our lives' trajectories forked and veered off in separate directions. I stayed at school; he left, and went to live on the other side of the country. He worked on shutdowns, at power plants and oil refineries, taking rooms above pubs or in cheap guesthouses. One day, he passed out at work. They took him to hospital, where they found a blood clot on his brain. When he came round after surgery – a shorn square of hair, two puckered sections of scalp stapled together – it was his landlady sitting next to his bed, not his mother. I listened to this, my mouth a slack 'O' of compassion. His life, as he described it, was one long round of privation and hardship. Like a Confederate boy soldier's, only with fewer drums and more choppers.

'I can't wait for you to meet *my* mum,' I said.

Absently, he ran a hand over his arm. I knew, without looking, he was touching the tattooed cursive of her name.

'I'll have to get rid of this before I do.'

'She knows you were married. We just have to say you were separated when we met.'

A lilac-haired girl swayed past us, in a vapour trail of scent. His eyes tracked her across the room.

'You'd look good, dressed up like that. We should go to the races. I'll wear a suit and a waistcoat. You can wear heels and a dress. I'll buy you one.'

I frowned. My miniature selves frowned back.

'What's wrong with the way I dress now?'

'Nothing. But at the races, everyone dresses up. I'd be in a suit and a waistcoat. You'd be in a dress and some heels. We'd look *class*.'

'I don't wear high heels. They're a plot against women. They mean you can't run away from men.'

He pulled me towards him. He smelled sweet. Aftershave,

fabric conditioner. Tequila-laced beer on his breath. Beneath that, the unmitigated sugar of his skin.

'Now why would you want to run away from me?'

The night swelled around us, and closed in. As it turned out, my snippy generalising at the casino was correct. The music they played in bars really *was* like early garage, so much so they could mix early garage into it. Only it had house's exultant pianos, those rumbling Italianate vamps that youths from post-industrial towns are predisposed to like, what I always classed as a north-western sound, without knowing why. Even now, those chords produced a plangent lifting in my chest, a sense that London had made me an exile in my own country. Being here made me see that life outside the city was as varied and continuous as life within. More so, in fact. And I had lately lost my home. But then I made his love the organising principle of my life. In that respect, at least, he had become my home.

*

At the flat, we left the windows open. As the light faded, his looks took on a generic, mutable quality. Stripped of his tracksuit in the semi-darkness, he could have been any one of my teenage boyfriends. I had definitely reverted to type with him, though it was a type so old, I'd almost forgotten it was mine. And the sex had a teenage flavour too, in that it was clumsy and disorganised, and I couldn't articulate what was wrong, or how to fix it. Twenty years since I'd dumped my virginity at the edge of a field, with all the ceremony of someone fly-tipping an old fridge, and my sexual responses were still a mystery to me.

I couldn't *say* what I wanted, because what I wanted resided deep down, in a place under language, a register that lost everything in translation. Words failed me here as they'd never failed me before, so I resorted to a cryptic system of shrugs and peeved silences, which he tried to decode, and could not. Away from him, I turned into a furtive, inveterate masturbator, an obsessed and needy correspondent. When we were together, I found myself scheming, trying to get out of it. Except there was no getting out of it. Sex was part of the compact we struck, the day he left, when he called to debrief me and said in a quavering voice: *You better love me, after all of this.* And I did love him, so took some pleasure in his, in watching his white beauty in the mirrored wardrobe, and itemising what later, I'd try to recall. Sweat-stiffened hair. Double-textured skin. Narrow gap between his teeth, visible as his mouth fell open.

Now, he put his hand over my mouth, a sign, somehow established and agreed upon that first night, that he was about to come. My earliest impressions of him were unchanged; he really *did* get harder than other men, and these erections were slower to subside. My tongue probed his fingers for the ring no longer there. I could still taste metal, but that was my own ferrous imprint: I was at the end of my period. In the mirror, his lips moved. He appeared to be saying something.

'What?'

'Your pussy. It's so tight.'

I used to like hearing him say this. Lately, it depressed me. It made me consider the impossible, Escheresque arc of male desire, the built-in obsolescence of the female body. If a man loved a woman, he'd want her to have his child. And when she gave him that child, he'd thank her by fucking a newer woman, with an unspent vagina, a cervix still intact. Some of this showed on my face. I knew this because I could see myself. He liked to watch us in the mirror. I was less keen. Something about the surface of the glass distorted our reflections.

'What's up?' he said.

'Nothing.'

'Are you worrying?'

'Maybe.'

'What about?'

'Stuff.'

He eased himself out of me. He was still hard, though I assumed he'd finished. I could feel a trail of rapidly cooling semen on my thigh.

'You never need worry about us. I want to be with you forever.'

'I'm sure you said the same to Rachel, once.'

'I *didn't.*'

'I'm pretty sure it's in the marriage vows.'

He put his arms around my waist and pulled me back against him. He ran so hot it was quite uncomfortable to share a bed with him in summer. Touching his leg, or the strip of skin below his ribs, was like brushing up against a radiator.

'We should have a baby.'

His lips were next to my ear, so I felt, rather than heard, him say the words. They were a ripple of sensation over my skin.

'Because settling down and having babies worked out so well for you last time?'

'It would be different with you.'

'It would. I'd make a terrible mother.'

'*Behave.* You'd make a great mam, you.'

It was part of my fascination for him that I'd managed to evade responsibility all my adult life. In his town, women had finished their families by the age of twenty-five.

'I'd be really short-tempered and inconsistent. And I wouldn't be able to help with its maths homework.'

'Maths was my best subject at school.'

I turned to see his face. His pupils were huge and oily. Only the finest rim of blue was visible around the black. He looked drugged. Maybe he was. Every relationship has its secrets. Patches of elision and deceit, like smudges on a scan.

'It would have awful hair. Wavy and thin. The worst of both worlds.'

'He'll be posh like his mam. Little like his dad. Messy-haired like both of us.'

We lay quietly for a while, listening to the keening of the gulls. I thought this was more or less how I'd pictured it, when possessing him was an insurmountable ambition, and all I had to sustain me was a belief in stories, and the suspicion he was lonelier than he was letting on. Leaving. Being left. He used to turn the corner at passport control, and I'd feel despair rise and rise within me, until it threatened to topple over and engulf everything.

After he left, I'd go and sit in the toilets and torment myself with contingencies, the only witness to my tears a punning recruitment poster tacked to the back of the stall (*Not feeling so flush?*). What if his chopper ditched, or he inhaled a cloud of condensate, or he slipped on a walkway and fell into the sea? What if his wife found out, or his interest waned, or he decided the risks were too high, the rewards too scant? *What if, what if?*

Crying over a married man when you've entered into an affair is like slamming your fingers in a car door, then complaining that it hurts. But it did hurt, more as time went on. The pain was integral to our design, so much so I sometimes wondered what we'd be without it. And now we were without it. Though hurt of this strain is never really eradicated. It's viral, and gets passed on.

'Are you glad we met?' he said.

'Yes. I'm glad I was burgled. I'm glad I lost my book. I'm glad I came here. If I didn't, I never would have found you.'

This was our catechism, our paean to fate's vectors: recited before bed, before parting, over the phone, on text. Each of us knew our lines, and recited our part.

'Are *you* glad we met?'

'Yes. I'm glad I got bumped that day. I'm glad you came and spoke to me. I'm glad that lad called you a bad word, because it meant we got to have the night together.'

I thought I would never get used to his being in my bed. That he was here now, that he would continue to be here, not just tomorrow, but for a numberless amount of days, stretching on into the future, felt miraculous.

I no longer put perfume of tuberose and amber in my hair.

I no longer wrote our initials on the steamed-up glass of the shower screen, or bound them with a circle.

I slept naked, and answered his texts straight away.

I was on a winning streak and winners have no need for the occult. I'd got what I wanted, what I'd secretly hoped for since the first day we met. And all I'd had to do was hold my nerve.

You've got no chance of getting me on a short leash. I've worked away forever, me. I've been doing this job eight year. Soon as I hit eighteen, that was it. It was my first job. I don't know nowt else. When I got with her, she had to adapt to my lifestyle, not the other way around. I go from country to country; I can be away nine weeks, ten weeks. I get back and for the first four days I turn my phone off. I don't see her. Obviously, I say hello, but we're struggling. It takes me so long to get used to being at home.

SIX

BRENT FIELD

'Why do you have to go now?'

'If I don't go now, I won't have the chance to talk to him again.'

Caden was ironing a polo shirt, a wounded expression on his face. If he was shocked to learn I didn't own a television, he'd been scandalised to hear I didn't have an iron, and marched out that same morning to rectify the situation. Ironing was a recurring *leitmotif* in his stories. He was still smarting over the way Rachel had scrunched his clothes into little balls, then hurled them into bin bags.

'I wouldn't have arranged it, if I'd known you were going to be here.'

He had arrived on the doorstep the day before, without warning. No one in the city had my address, so when the intercom buzzed, I went to the window. A white Range Rover was parked outside, its engine still running. He was standing at the door, his kit bag on the floor beside him. I ran down the stairs, as if we'd been separated for months rather than days.

'I didn't know, I didn't know,' I said childishly, covering the side of his face with kisses. 'I didn't know you were coming.'

'I know you didn't,' he said, walking me backwards, his hand at my throat. My head hit the wall with a light crack. 'That was the idea.'

He enjoyed situations like this, where he knew something I didn't, and could appear, as if by magic, and rewrite the course of my day. He liked surprises, big gestures and snap decisions; he was faddy, like Toad of Toad Hall. I liked surprises too, but found it difficult to keep him entertained. I felt as if I'd coaxed a wild animal into the flat: thrilled to see him out of context, guiltily aware I lacked the means to make him comfortable.

I had never met a person so easily bored, or harder to occupy. He had no interests apart from going to the gym. He knew a few men up here (occasionally, as we walked through town, he'd nod austerely at one on the street), but no one he could properly call a friend. The only books he read were biographies of drug barons and mafia dons (both in short supply at my flat); the only films he liked were biopics of noted football hooligans. We went to the cinema once, to see the new *Mad Max*, but he was up and down so often, buying beer and popcorn and sweets, he missed half of it. He was visibly uncomfortable in restaurants, growing flushed and tongue-tied over the menu, his finger moving over the page as if it were written in braille. He was fit, but urban by instinct, and pulled a face when I suggested a walk. I was diverted to find out, during this same conversation, that he could barely swim. He looked nonplussed when I asked if he might be in the wrong job. 'My job isn't swimming,' he said.

We compromised by hiring a car and driving to the Highlands. We stopped at Cairn Gorm and took the funicular to the top.

Freezing sheets of mist rolled off the mountain and down the chute, like dry ice. The sky had the sallow look that usually presages snow. This high, there were no seasons.

The slanting carriage was hauled backwards, along the narrow escarpment and up into the mist. Panels of flint and lichened rock slid past the window. Caden sat beside me, emanating the wordless satisfaction of one proved right. He had wanted to go shopping again, and I insisted this would be more fun. We might see a hare or a ptarmigan, I told him by way of inducement. The funicular drew to a halt and the doors opened with a hiss. We went and stood on the viewing platform. I peered over the edge, light-headed with altitude. There were no hares or ptarmigans. There was just scree, patches of moss and blasted vegetation. The mountain cast a deep bowl of shadow, so the fields below looked cursed, as if they'd been plunged into perpetual winter. It was very cold.

'Shall we go home?' I said. Caden's expression was inscrutable, beneath the mirrored glasses. 'I'm not bothered,' he said. 'Whatever you like.'

The more I saw of him, the more I noticed this malleability. He was like water. He assumed the form of whomever he was with at the time. After a few days with me, he'd parrot my opinions. After a few days at home, he'd come back full of new ideas, presumably cribbed from his friends. I was starting to realise that much of what I'd thought of as his personality was just stuff I'd dreamt up during his long absences. In the same way I used to fill in the blank oval of his face, with features *like* his, but not his; I'd created a character that alluded to him, while being subtly different. His real character was harder to pin down. He had no principles or politics to speak of. There was nothing he'd die in a ditch for, no side worth taking but his own. Unusually for an only child, he didn't just dislike his own company, but seemed to fear it, and was thrown into panic by the prospect of spending time alone. Though he supported my writing in principle, in practice he stopped me working.

He pulled his shirt on and walked over to the window. The air shimmered. Across the street, the buildings looked silvered. There was a sheen to the stone, a metallic seam that only showed up in strong sunlight.

'Looks mafting out there.'

'It's meant to be hot today.'

I put my arms around his waist and tucked my chin into his shoulder. For a moment, his hand tightened on my arm, then went slack.

'Don't be long,' he said. 'I'll miss you.'

*

The man I was meeting worked on the Brent Field. He was a kind of Typhoid Mary, having worked on the site of several accidents, always escaping unscathed. He was staying in a large, anonymous hotel behind Holburn Junction. The lobby was a columnar space several floors high. Its windows were covered in a kind of mesh, which muted the daylight and cast everything in a cool, neutral gloom. I took a booth, upholstered the same indeterminate shade, and waited for him to appear. There was some splashy abstract art on the walls, and a long, curved reception desk at the back of the room. People were moving about in the shadowy recess behind it, like stagehands in the wings of a theatre. No one showed any inclination to come out.

The meeting had been arranged by a mutual acquaintance, and this connection, coupled with the blandly corporate look of the building, made me feel as if I were the one being interviewed. After a few minutes, a man stepped out of the lift. He was small and powerfully built, with red hair and a full red beard. His cheeks were round and rosy, and his teeth pushed against his upper lip, so his mouth didn't quite close, giving him a look of breathy suspense. He sat down opposite me and rubbed his hands together, in what might have been an expression of anticipation, or an attempt to get warm. The weather was close, and the air conditioning was turned up high.

'So you're the writer?'

I nodded shyly.

'I've often thought I should write a book.'

'You should,' I said. 'Why not?'

This was my default response to a statement I heard at least once a day, sometimes more, and the opposite of what I thought. What I really thought was that if people knew how difficult it was, no one would attempt it, that there must be a conspiracy of silence amongst authors, since this misconception that everyone had a book in them was so widely held. Usually, at this point in the conversation, the person talking about writing would say he didn't really have the time, I'd agree that it *was* time consuming, and the subject would be dropped. But this man surprised me, by pushing three cellophane wallets across the table. They were three stories from his life, that I could use, or not, as I saw fit. It had taken him several days to write them up, but he'd found the process curiously therapeutic, so in a way, they'd already served their purpose.

'If nothing else,' he said, 'they might give you a laugh.'

I thanked him, and tucked the wallets into my bag. I asked where he was going that afternoon. The Brent Charlie, he answered, with a grimace. Two and a half hours in the chopper. Three, in an oncoming wind. If you had the misfortune to be sat next to a big guy – and for some reason, there *were* a lot of big guys on the Brent Field – you'd spend the flight perched on the edge of the seat. From the Charlie, he'd fly to the Alpha. He was a plumber, and the role was peripatetic, so over the course of one trip he'd work his way around all four platforms.

'Which one's your favourite?' I said idly. I was thinking out loud, as I did more and more these days, but he surprised me a second time, by treating the question with more seriousness than it deserved.

'Probably the Alpha. It's small, there's not so many guys on it, and it's just been done up. I used to like the Delta. It's going through decommissioning just now, so the legs will be cut off in six months' time. And then the Delta will be no more.'

'Which one's the worst?'

'The Charlie's got the most people on it, and only a tiny wee gym. The Bravo's bad for arseholes.'

His voice was low and sleepy, as if lulled by its own susurration. Some of his sentences petered out into nothing. At other times he'd pause, before picking up where he left off.

'The best rig I ever worked on was the Lomond. The atmosphere there was always good. The Tartan was probably the worst. On the Tartan, the cabins had two bunk beds and a zed bed, for a fifth person. You had three guys on days, two on nights, and one bathroom between the two rooms. *Ten* people to a bathroom. It was wet the whole time. I've worked on the Claymore as well. That's a disaster of a rig.'

I wondered if his choice of words was deliberate.

'James said you were on Piper Alpha.'

'I was. Only one trip. I was twenty, and *very* excited to be earning one pound eighty an hour. It was a massive platform, an old rusting bucket, even then. It's like stepping off a bus, then seeing it go off a cliff. You think, "I was on that place and now it's at the bottom of the sea." There but for the grace of God, you know?

You read the names, looking for someone you know. My old fore-man, Jim McCulloch … he was on there.'

He sighed, and looked past me. A waitress had emerged from the back of the room. She was dressed in a drooping dark tunic, and trousers so long they covered her shoes, so she looked as though she was gliding about on casters. She took our order and slid back across the room, towards the desk. Once she was gone, he started talking again.

'There's a veneer of safety now. But the way a multinational views safety off West Africa is different from the way it views safety in the North Sea. You see pictures of guys welding with cling film wrapped around their eyes. If someone gets injured out there, it won't make the news, it won't affect share prices. Or is that too cynical?'

'You're asking the wrong person.'

He smiled, displaying large, rounded teeth. Many of the men I'd met looked worn out by the physicality of their work, but this man emitted an air of wholesome good health. He must have been in his late forties, at least, to have worked on Piper Alpha, but in the dim light of the lobby, he appeared almost ageless.

'We've had a lot of deaths on the Brents over the years. We had the Chinook disaster … forty-five people who'd left the Brent Delta. There were two guys killed down the leg of the Brent Bravo. During the last downturn.'

The man explained that oil companies were expected to deliver nominations – specific quantities of oil and gas – to the grid. Failure to do so incurred penalties. But there is a constant tension between production and compliance. Platforms become fatigued over time. Battered by the elements, their structures need contin-ued maintenance. Routine maintenance often puts operations on hold, and during downturns, companies will deploy quick fixes. In 1999, it was alleged that Shell had a protocol known as TFA: Touch

Fuck All. Permits apparently came with TFA scrawled across them, meaning workers should leave equipment alone, rather than risk a shutdown (though this was denied by Shell). Shell commissioned an internal audit, which corroborated the allegations and recommended immediate intervention. But the auditor was transferred, and the report did not surface again until 2006, shortly before a Fatal Accident Inquiry into the Brent Bravo deaths.

One day, the man said, two workers were sent to the bottom of the Bravo's leg to investigate a leaking pipe. At that point, there were many leaking pipes on the platform. Many grazes and abrasions in its fabric. The bottom of the leg was a stinking, horrible place. Poorly lit and dank. The men had to stand on a metal grate above a stagnant pool of bilge and patch the leak up with a piece of neoprene and a jubilee clip. What they didn't know was that the clear, scentless substance leaking from the pipe was liquid hydrocarbon. As it hit the grating below it began to evaporate, swelling back around them in a doughnut cloud.

The alarms activated and the valves designed to divert gas away from the plant and up towards the flare kicked into gear. All except one, which failed. The system hadn't been tested for a while. To test is to touch. The men tried to make it up the stairs but they were too far down. They were asphyxiated in minutes.

Shell pleaded guilty to safety lapses and was fined £900,000; a little less than it earned in an hour. No substantive evidence of the TFA protocol was offered in court, but the company admitted: 'There is still much we need to do.'

The man paused and looked out towards the street. People were walking past, pale silhouettes against the mesh. The traffic at Holburn Junction was a faint hum.

'There was another one,' he said. 'A few years back now. On the Delta. A man filled his pockets with tools and jumped off the side.'

I stared. My mouth hung open in sympathy with his.

'I've heard that story so many times. I assumed it was an urban myth.'

'Oh *no*. It really did happen. I saw him half an hour before. I passed him in the corridor and said, "All right Jimmy, how you doing?" He never took me on, just walked right past. I didn't think anything of it. Then they started putting tannoys out, asking him to report to heli admin. I said, "Maybe he's jumped off the platform." As a joke, you know? Can you imagine how I felt afterwards? When the alarms went off: *Man Missing*. Then the story came out. He was very money-orientated. He worked a lot of overtime. This is only what I've heard, mind. But he was the tightest guy in the world. Money was king. I think that played a part in it. His wife was leaving him, and she was going to get the house. It drove him mad. Perhaps he thought that with killing himself, she wouldn't get anything. Insurance doesn't pay out for suicide.'

'Divorce does funny things to people.'

'Aye.' He moved back in his seat to make space for the waitress, as she set our drinks down. 'That it does.'

*

Caden had been busy in my absence. He'd stripped the beds, washed the sheets and hung them over the doors to dry, so the air in the flat felt faintly clammy.

The dishes were stacked in the cupboards, the floors had been vacuumed. In the spare room, his clothes were laid out on the bed, as if arranged with a set square. His kitbag and shoes (stiff little pumps of blue and red leather that looked like children's bowling shoes) were stowed by the door. He was the neatest man I'd ever known, unable to rest until everything was in its proper place. I told him he could keep some clothes here, that the wardrobe in the spare room was his if he wanted it. He was oddly resistant to this idea, bringing only four shirts and a pair of shorts. He preferred to travel light, he said. Once, when he was in the shower, I went rooting in his bag. I don't know what I was looking for, only that I was obeying a powerful instinct to search, and this felt more forgivable than going through his phone. It was empty, except for a bottle of water and his Vantage card. I sat back on my heels, turning the card over and over, as if it held some encrypted information.

At first, I put it down to his spending half his life in a confined space. As the summer wore on, it became clear these efforts to impose order on his surroundings were a reaction to his affairs spinning out of control. To no one's surprise but his own, Rachel didn't buy his reasons for leaving (which were no reasons, just a nebulous conviction there was 'something' wrong with their marriage). But the speed at which she found me shocked us both.

That night, we lay in bed clinging to each other, the covers pulled over our heads. This is ridiculous, I thought. We are *literally* hiding under the duvet. There were two of us, and only one of her, but the force of her fury made it feel like we were outnumbered. Everything we did was done at counterpoint to an insistent, insectoid buzzing. His phone. Then mine. Then his again. Then mine. In the flat, my phone was synched to my laptop, so both devices shrilled simultaneously, making me feel doubly hectored.

Whenever I turned either on, a soft flurry of abuse hit the screen. *Slag. Slut. Whore. Tart. Dropped ur knickers. Spread ur legs. Filthy bitch. Dirty cunt.* I was a slapper, who hurt innocent children. A tramp, who broke up happy families. A succubus, who used bad magic to mock up the luridly green grass on my side of the fence. At times, she'd call repeatedly, or send seven texts in a row. At others, she'd fall mysteriously silent, traceable only by her credit card activity. Caden scrolled through these statements, smiling grimly. Only he was allowed to spend like this. They had a fifties-style set-up at home, where he gave her a monthly allowance, like an employee, or a child. And there was something transactional about her talk, a till ring always audible beneath the threats and imprecations.

I was a cheap slut. The affair was a cheap thrill. She was worth ten of me. He couldn't even get himself an upgrade! He'd traded her in for a ropey old tart.

For Rachel, there were two types of women, Good Wives and Slags. Slags could be sub-divided into Little Slags (nubile cuties in small dresses, who went out drinking with the aim of getting themselves pregnant), and fully realised Slags. Good Wives were all the same: perfect. 'Tell your wife her internalised misogyny is showing again,' I'd say mildly, handing Caden my phone.

Inside, my temper banged. I tried blocking her number, but it was no use. She just withheld it, or used one of her seemingly inexhaustible supply of burners. Already, I was feeling nostalgic for those prelapsarian weeks before she knew my name. Once she had my name, it was the work of a few hours to get everything else. She kept calling Caden with new bits of information, as if I were an exam she was sitting, and she was hell-bent on getting an A. She trawled the internet for the most unflattering pictures of me, which she sent to him (scathing captions attached). She read all my articles. Somehow, she got my address, an address no one had, not even my mother.

She frightened me, though I didn't like to admit it. It was a fear as old as school itself: girl gangs, focused female animus. In photos, she exuded the lean, stringy menace, the superb physical confidence, of an undefeated welterweight. More than her body, her bearing suggested she could bang. She regarded the camera coolly, as if daring the viewer to keep looking. I could never scroll through her Instagram without feeling that she somehow *knew*. It added a frisson to my spying. Her account was public, as one might expect from a person trying to convince her ex she was *2 blessed 2 b stressed*, and predictably composed (two parts carefree selfies to one part sour memes). Karma was a favoured theme: every dog had its day. Apex predators would soon be food for worms. Time was the only currency with any real-world value.

Caden was obviously the kind of cheat driven by a greed for variety, the same that once made me covet a brunette Skipper to add to my troupe of blonde Barbies. His wife and I were as different as two people could be. She had large, light eyes, and a lot of shiny red hair – a darker, richer red than I'd imagined – which she wore piled up, to emphasise a long, slender neck. Her face was a contoured heart, with a high domed forehead and a tiny chin. Square-tipped acrylics. Spindly heels. The high finish of a woman who didn't have to work. Her head was too big for her body, and there was one dress in particular – a narrow blue sheath that resolved itself in a choker-like tie at the throat – that made her look like one of those bottle-necked Cluedo characters.

All her pictures shared this hyperreal aspect; her eyes infinitesimally larger than actual eyes, her skin a soft-focus smear. Her clothes were less like real clothes than little costumes. Autumnal Rachel, in buff Uggs and chunky knit, strolling through the woods, a twin on each arm. Pilates Rachel, in grey yoga pants, pink Nikes, a toning pink bubble tea in her tiny, pink-nailed hand. Races Rachel, in decorous print dress and platforms high as chopines. Wedding Rachel, in a lunatic confection of frills, froth and furbelows, random pin tucks and senseless sections of asymmetry. She made an unsmiling bride, rising severely from the stiff tulle bodice like a Viking longboat's figurehead, breasting through a storm-tossed sea. Perhaps she had a premonition that her young man would not give her much to smile about.

I did this snooping in secret. He got twitchy at the mere mention of us making contact. I wasn't allowed to answer her calls, or reply to her texts, no matter how provocative they were. He insisted this was for my own good. Dealing with her was dirty, mannish work, akin to changing the oil in a car or taking the bins out, and I wasn't up to the job. *She's a nightmare*, he'd say with a shudder, like a child recalling an actual nightmare. *You don't want to know.* But I did want to know. I did. I was intrigued as to what she was finding to say, during her seventh, eighth, ninth call of the day. He answered these calls as faithfully as when they were together, jumping up from his seat and scuttling out of the room.

I followed him once, though what I witnessed told me nothing. He was leaning against the kitchen counter (brows raised, expression bland), while a tinny stream of invective leached from the phone. As I closed the door behind me, I heard him sigh *haway*. Most of the time, it felt like she was in the flat with us. By sheer force of will, she had made herself the central concern of our lives.

Caden – who used to look at me blankly when I mentioned her, as if he knew no one of that name – now talked of little else. I found these conversations simultaneously boring and stressful, like maths, and wished they would stop. Every day, there was some development, a new proffer or withdrawal, another friend conscripted onto her side. Like a sinking ship, their divorce was dragging people down with it; anyone close enough to read the writing on the hull was getting sucked into the undertow.

'Rachel's just text,' he called, as I walked through the door. 'To say she hates us.'

I dropped my keys on the table and picked up my post. The racing was on, and a list of runners had been scribbled on the back of a brown envelope.

'Both of us? Or just you?'

'She said it was a cunt's move, calling from the rig. She said I should have done the decent thing and told her to her face.'

Since I agreed with Rachel on this, I said nothing. I went into the bedroom, took my dress off and pinned my hair up. The flat was uncomfortably hot. Ours was a new enough relationship that walking back into a room in my underwear could, under normal circumstances, be interpreted as a come-on, but Caden was too preoccupied to notice.

'She says I'm a little man, in every way.'

I fetched two beers from the fridge. It was empty, apart from a few scattered garlic cloves and some damp thyme. My efforts to convince him I'd make as good a wife as Rachel had lapsed, and my housekeeping had reverted to its slovenly default. I'd lost all enthusiasm for cooking, since he was so fussy. The list of foods he didn't like was long and exhaustive (including, but not limited to: fish, apart from fish in batter; seafood; cheese; pâté; egg yolks; tofu; black pudding; chorizo; hummus; cucumber; peas; cream; cream-based sauces; porridge; gherkins; olives; yogurt; avocado; coffee; wine), and I wasn't prepared to waste hours in the kitchen, if all he was going to do was push the meal around his plate. Mostly, we lived on children's party food – sausage rolls, crisps, chicken drumsticks, chocolate – which added to the interim feel of our arrangements, the sense we were just playing house.

'You're not a little man,' I said, handing him a beer. 'You're a nice person who's made an unpopular decision.'

'The girls don't want to see me.'

'They'll hate you for a bit. And then they'll come round.'

I pulled the papers from my bag and sat down next to him. His breath was sweet and boozy. I wondered how long he'd been drinking.

'What's that?'

'A tale of marital discord.'

'Whose?'

'The man I met before.'

The writing was full of ellipses, unnecessary dashes, arbitrary spaces, reminiscent of the pauses and elisions in his speech.

'His wife was a bitch.'

'You're only getting one side of the story there.'

'True. But he was a nice man.'

'He'll be lying, to get your sympathy.'

'Not everyone tells lies.'

'Everyone offshore does.'

'He was on the Delta when that lad jumped off.'

'Yeah, right.'

'Why would he lie?'

'To impress you.'

'What's impressive about that?'

Caden didn't answer, but nodded authoritatively at the television. The racing was over and the news was showing a clip of some men in battle fatigues and balaclavas, waving a black flag.

'Bet you love these.'

'What makes you think I'd like Isis?'

'You probably think it's they parents' fault.'

'I'm actually more right wing than you give me credit for.'

'You probably want them to move over here and sign on.'

'I'm very hot on law and order.'

'Give them a nice six-bedroom house for all they kids.'

He stretched out beside me. I smoothed his hair back from his forehead. He had a pertly consistent face. Time had abraded his skin, but left the underlying structure intact. He would be instantly identifiable in baby photos, exempt from those party games where pictures of mystery infants are glued onto sugar paper.

'Of the two women in your life, only one acts like she was raised in a Levantine shame culture. And it isn't me.'

On cue, my phone vibrated:

I no were u work. I can course u alot of problems.

'I fancy she'd do rather well under Sharia law.'

The lavender evening was thickening. A car went past, trailing crystalline fragments of two-step. The prostitutes on the corner had shed their parkas and jeans, and were dressed, for once, like prostitutes of popular imagination. This district was usually quiet in the evenings, but people were out late, their curfews extended by the heat.

Caden flicked disconsolately between channels. It pained him to know there were people in the world who thought him imperfect. I'd taken him for an adult because he earned a lot of money, but he was like me. Critique gave him heartburn. Credit checks, tax returns, medicals, appraisal in any form. In giving the grownups the slip, we'd created a power vacuum. In the afternoons, we went back to bed, as if we lived in a Latin country rather than a chill Presbyterian port. And in the mornings, I woke up feeling guilty. We consumed endless trashy television, with special account given to the lower-tier reality shows, where teak-coloured men in peg trousers buttonholed interchangeable women for stilted 'chats'. ITV2 was a Möbius strip of mindless content. Cousins of the TOWIE cast, people affiliated with the Kardashians, spinoffs of spinoffs.

'Leave it,' I said, as he alighted on *Love Island*.

Said and I had become mildly obsessed with this programme. The premise was stupid, but at some point we stopped watching ironically, and became sincerely involved. I'd been initiating him into the mysteries of *That's You*, a game of mine and my sister's invention. While he got the general idea, he was yet to master its nuances.

Already, those first few weeks in Aberdeen – the era of Said and the back to back – had taken on the tint of history. I missed them. I missed their flat. There was a lived-in texture to the gentle sag of the sofa, the planed reddish wood of the window frames. It reminded me of my cousins' house, which was to do with the old-fashioned coral and green colour scheme on the upholstery, and the faint smell of wood smoke in the rooms. I sought to memorialise the friendship by making Caden watch *Love Island* with me, though the tenor of his commentary was different, so I felt their loss more keenly.

Caden could not cultivate the necessary distance. The men looked like him, with large biceps, cut obliques and sleeve tattoos. The women looked like Rachel, with fronded eyelashes, pearlescent browbones and waist-length hair. They looked like each other too, and like the models in the advert breaks. Their cosmetic similarities vitiated any racial difference, so they appeared to have come from one family, a line of full-lipped, snub-nosed, taupe-skinned Amazons. They were all the same shape, and struck the same curvilinear poses – backs arched, arses thrust outwards – so sitting down, they resembled chess knights, or seahorses. They were self made women, and like self-made people in the past, they'd never escape their origins. They could make a career of sorts, but a gulf always remained between reality stars and the other kind.

On screen, a boy was being driven to the villa in an open-topped Jeep. His profile was so taut and smooth it looked like it was carved from wax. He was narrating his progress up the drive, in droning voiceover.

'I'm my own brand. I'm going to show the girls a new kind of guy. People look up to me, they like my style. They like the way

I go about life. A typical night out for me is the best place, the best drinks, the best girls. I haven't chased girls for years. The way my image is, they come to me ...'

My phone vibrated again. It was a text from Said.

He's you, it said.

*

The last dream I had before waking, and the most vivid, in the way of late-phase dreams, was that Aberdeen was occupied by Russia. Or at least, a race of Russian speakers. It was snowing, the bright, white, powdery snow of Christmas cards, not the wet, sleety kind that turns grey on contact with the pavement. People were dashing about in chinchilla hats and long wool coats. Signs were written in Cyrillic. I was the only person in the city who didn't have a word of Russian, and Said was acting as my transla-tor. He was leading me around by the elbow, as though I was blind. And I *did* feel incapacitated. I'd lost my powers of commu-nication. All around me, people were in possession of knowledge I needed, and didn't have. We met the back to back in a high-ceilinged room hung with heavy red brocade, which was either a haberdashery department or a hotel suite. In the closing moments of the dream, he told me that the correct way to pronounce an accented word in Russian was to smile.

When a person appears in your dream, he went to sleep thinking of you.

It felt so real that when I got up, I half expected to see snow on the ground outside. Caden was already awake, pacing the flat, his phone pressed to his ear. He was flying home later, to fetch the rest of his clothes and move them to his mother's house. His remaining possessions (the eight televisions, the 5 series, the biog-raphies of career criminals, the painting of the white-haired sylph at sunset) were to be forfeited. 'We're not,' he said, when I asked how they planned to divide them. 'I'm only thirty. I've got time to start again.'

I followed him into the kitchen. I wanted to tell him about the dream, to stabilise its essence before it disappeared. Then I saw his face. Always pale, he was paper white with shock. He held the phone to his chest, and briefed me through blanched lips. It was his mother. A letter had arrived from Rachel's solicitor. Her decision to stay at home for a decade had turned her into a third dependent. She required support for the next fifteen years, possibly forever. Irrespective of her ambitions before marriage, in divorce she would be treated as a thwarted careerist, and compensated accordingly. She wanted four thousand pounds a month. I said the second thing that occurred to me (the first – *I thought you said she didn't know anything about the business account* – didn't seem very helpful).

'It's just a proffer. Her lawyer will have told her to get in there and get everything, while you're feeling guilty.'

He gave me an injured look.

'She'll get fuck all. I'm moving my wages into an umbrella fund. The lads at work all do it. Why should I pay her to sit on her arse all day? If she wants money, she can get a job.'

We were both quiet on the way to the airport, sunk in our own separate thoughts. As we neared Dyce, he reached for my hand. The sleeves of his jumper were pushed back, as if in anticipation of the dirty work that waited for him at the other end. He smiled at me, but it was no good. The route must have activated a reflex, and I felt myself sliding into a mood of punchy, irrational abnegation. All morning it had been like this, our moods alternating, each of us trying to compensate for the other's bad temper, as if we were on a seesaw.

'I'm coming back, you know.'

'You're not, I know you're not. She's going to guilt you into staying. You're *weak*, when it comes to her.'

'I'm coming back and getting you pregnant. Then when your book makes loads of money, I can give up work, and look after messy hair.'

A wedge of farmland ran parallel to the road. I considered the rows of grey cabbages, the serried polythene tunnels. Why did he keep going on about the book? *He* should go and write a book, if he thought it was such a brilliant idea.

I tried to manage his expectations by dropping dispiriting statistics about writers' earnings into the conversation, and reminding him that in my best, most profitable weeks I'd barely grazed his day rate, but he remained disproportionately impressed I'd had a job at all.

'I can't write any more. I haven't written a single decent sentence since I moved here.'

It was the first time I'd articulated this thought, and saying it out loud, I realised it was true. Tears pricked my eyes, sending warm rills through my careful make-up. Caden spat on the pad of his thumb and wiped them away.

'You'll get it back.'

'Are you really going to move your money offshore?'

'If she carries on like this.'

'What about the girls?'

'The twins won't want for nothing.'

'Caden, they can't *eat* their iPads.'

My phone buzzed in my bag.

How u find them is how u loose them!!!

He squeezed my hand.

'She'll stop soon. I promise.'

'I'm sick of her.'

'So am I.'

'I'm going to the police. This is harassment.'

'If you go to the police, you'll make it ten times worse. We had an affair. She's going to be pissed off.'

I snatched my hand back.

'I can't believe you're taking her side!'

'I'm not. But put yourself in her place. You stole her husband.'

'I didn't *steal* you. Why are you talking like her?'

The taxi drew up outside the airport. Our last moments had been wasted arguing about Rachel. Knowing how this would have pleased her, I made an effort to pull myself together. I took his hand and we walked into the building. Arrivals had the sad look of a sparsely attended party. I thought of last winter, days of scrappy, high-toned confidence. *End of March, everything will go back to normal.* But things had not gone back to normal. And they were set to get worse before they could get better. The North Sea was finished. That's what people were saying now. Commerce moves forward with the faithless trajectory of a shark, discarding what is old, outmoded, obsolete. We had a good run. But nothing lasts forever.

'Don't forget about me,' I said at passport control.

He tugged on the collar of my coat, as he used to, and put his lips against my temple.

'How could I?' he murmured into my hair.

I watched him go. He turned back once, and waved. It was the last time I ever saw him. What did I expect? It is terrible luck to watch a person leave.

*The majority of the crew will be Teesside. Teesside mafia.
Everybody knows everybody. They know who's willing to work.
They know who'll avoid it. When I first started out, there were
lads who'd never served their time, never done an apprenticeship,
and you could write a CV for them, put yourself down as a
reference, another mutual friend down as reference, and get them
a start offshore as a qualified technician or rigger. There are lads
who have no experience – none – who I know work offshore full
time, from a made-up CV and made-up references. Years ago, if
you went out and said 'Look, I've never done this before' and you
were honest with the people you were working with, they'd say
'Don't worry, we'll look after you'. They'd train you. And you'd
become that trade.*

SEVEN

PIPER BRAVO

'Where are you going?'

'Nowhere,' I said. 'Home.'

'Don't go yet,' the man said. 'Come and have a drink.'

I peered up at him, trying to get a read on his motives. He was a big man, not just tall but broad, with a thick pad of muscle across his shoulders that made him look hunchbacked. He wore a large, padded coat with a fur-trimmed hood, pulled up over a peaked cap. On the train, he said he used to box professionally, at welterweight, though I found it hard to believe he'd ever been light enough.

He'd got on at Darlington, and nodded at me from beneath his cap, as if we were already acquainted. The carriage was empty, like the airport, like the city itself that autumn, and when he started talking, somewhere after Berwick, there was a similar ease to it. He felt familiar, somehow. It was as if we'd talked before and were merely picking up where we left off. The borderlands whipped past the window, and the lights flicked on overhead, apparently activated by the gloom outside. The long nights came on quickly here.

By the time we got to Aberdeen, it was quite dark. I'd lost track of time over the summer. Things stopped running in chronological order. I raked over recent memories, so they often seemed more real, more substantive than the present, which had a hallucinatory feel. The days had been long, and the pitiless light blazed on outside as I moved through the season like a sleepwalker, barely registering events around me. My sister's baby shower; my cousin's birthday; a week in Ibiza. *Don't ruin this for her*, my mother warned me, in a low, firm voice, on the day of the shower. I was annoyed she'd said it, though in a way I felt like I *was* ruining it, that I was infecting the day with toxic juju, like a bad fairy left off a guest list. Relations between my sister and me had been scratchy for months. We were batting for opposing teams now. The house was full of her pregnant friends, stately and full-faced in their maxi-dresses, and I thought I could read pity in their expressions when they asked about the book.

In these circles, you were nothing if not half of a couple, and questions that didn't concern husband and home were white noise. They sat in the garden, playing baby-themed parlour games and cooing as my sister tore duck-print paper from her cache of gifts. Carabosse-like, I skulked in the spare room, drinking Campari and compulsively checking my phone.

This was in the immediate aftermath, when I thought I knew how things would go. I assumed shock was having an analgesic effect on Caden. Once the reality of life without me hit him, he'd be back. I found myself looking forward to the day as a child looks forward to Christmas. I anticipated the slew of miserable messages I'd receive, the way a child eyes up a stocking (unsure of the contents, suspecting she will like them).

But that day never came. When he completed a whole trip, spending three weeks at home and three at work, without calling once, I stopped hoping. He wasn't suffering like me, too proud and hurt to pick up the phone. He had redacted me from his life, from his history.

His wife showed more constancy. She put in a call every Saturday night, emboldened by a cocktail or two with 'the girlies'. She must think I'm stupid, I thought, watching the withheld number flash up on screen. She must not know about me: private caller ignorer *par excellence*. Although of course, she did know all about me, and had no reason to credit me with any intelligence. After a while, her calls stopped too. And then my final connection with that couple was severed forever.

I may have been a bit mad during that period. I became an obsessed archivist, an unhinged scholar, going over events in my mind, trying to retrace my steps, to pinpoint the moment I went wrong. I fixated on dates – on discarded train tickets and receipts, time stamps on texts, back issues of magazines in the doctor's waiting room – wishing myself back so I could correct my behaviour, drop all my bad habits in time. I cried so much, my cheeks were permanently smeared with aubergine mascara, like one of those Marian statues that weeps blood.

And there was something remarkable, something curious, about this extravagant, red-teared despair. People started to talk about me as if I wasn't there. My mother wondered aloud if I was having some sort of breakdown. Friends stared when they saw me, and said I needed to eat.

They didn't understand. I didn't have *time* to eat. I was too busy crying, and writing long, self-exculpatory emails that would never be sent, and spying online, trying to work out whether Caden was sending me messages, only in code. When I posted a photo of my friend and me at DC10 on Instagram, he uploaded a similar one within hours. *Look* at the composition, I told her. It's identical. We're both on holiday, we're both hugging a friend, we're both smiling. What *can* it mean? She squinted over my shoulder. He's wearing a vest, she said. How can you be in love with a man who wears a vest?

Was I still mad? I considered this as the man picked up my bag and swung it over his shoulder, and led me across the concourse. I was certainly desperate for company. The cumulative effect of so many days and weeks alone was beginning to weigh on me. I could go whole weekends now without speaking to anyone, except to thank cashiers for my change, or baristas for my coffee. Loneliness wasn't an abstract concept but an animate threat, one I had to keep a hair's breadth ahead of at all times, like the cartoon bird, its legs a whirring blur before the coyote's snapping jaws. So I followed him, without much thought, over the railway bridge, up a steep flight of stone steps and down a series of narrow entries. Having approached his hotel from the back, it was only when I saw the wrought-iron railings at the front that I realised where we were.

'I've been here before,' I said.

Been here before. That's what people kept saying about my sister's baby. She had large, dark eyes and a tiny strawberry mark on her cheek. The night I first met her, when everyone else had gone home, she started to cry. My sister and I looked at each other with undisguised panic; neither of us had any idea what to do. The baby lay across my knee, as hot and rigid as a poker, screaming and screaming. My sister danced above us uncertainly, waving a little bear on a string, like a witch doctor shaking a fetish. More often, the baby lay quietly in her crib, wearing a sombre expression. *Old soul*, everyone said. *She's been here before.*

I had actually been here before, though. This was the basement bar where I met Caden and Tyler, the day of the snow. The city was so small, I'd been everywhere twice. The past wasn't a foreign country to me but a nearby principality, with a shared language, and lax border control.

'Have you?'

The man glanced over his shoulder. He looked as if he didn't believe me.

'A while ago,' I amended. 'Last winter.'

I looked around, absorbing the realities of the room. It was cleaner, smaller, less run down than I remembered. There were several large flat screens, placed at intervals along the walls, showing highlights of a football match with the sound turned down. There were only two other customers, solitary drinkers, sitting separately at the bar. The shock I felt as I walked in, trying to square the space with my memory of it, reminded me of the slight scramble I used to make every time I saw Caden, reconciling the real him with the version that lived in my head.

A woman was raped here, they said. Last summer; not the one just gone. During a long, hot week in July, when the mists wouldn't clear. Crews arrived in the city to find it bottlenecked. Flights cancelled, hotels full. No one came prepared. The shops were stripped of cheap shorts, T-shirts, sunglasses. The pubs were full all day. There was a festal atmosphere in town: the heat, the crowds, the jettisoned routine. The woman went upstairs with a man she'd met that night, and they found her a few hours later in the gutter outside. The city ran on rumour, stories were fed into its system of whisper and cross-reference, then churned out with new details. But several people had told me this one, and the details never changed, so I assumed it must be true.

'I'm just taking my bag up to the room,' the man said. 'Do you want me to take yours too?'

I was unsure how to respond to this. It occurred to me I could be offended by his presumption, but I was chiefly concerned with not causing offence myself.

'No,' I said. 'Thank you.'

When he came back downstairs, I asked him where he was going.

'The Bruce. Not my favourite. Last time, we were stuck in Sumburgh two days. There's nowt up there except cows, and weird locals. They've all got frizzy hair and bad shoes. Clogs, if you like. Not that I'm a fashionista.'

I smiled at this. It seemed a word lifted from someone else's vocabulary. Though he was obviously attached to his coat, which he'd kept on. The fur looked thick and lustrous, and the coat's obvious expense set him apart from his surroundings. I wondered if he thought I was going to try and steal it, that this whole interview was some sort of long con, and I was just waiting for my chance to roll it up into a ball, slip out of the bar and vanish into the night.

'Before the Bruce, I was on Piper Bravo. Before that, I was in the Falklands.'

'What was that like?'

'Oh, horrible. Horrible! I've worked in some of the roughest places in the world. Saudi: that's a shithole. It's hot, but not a *nice* hot. But the Falklands was the worst. The rig was halfway between the islands and the South Pole. Bang in the middle. It could go from fifteen degrees to minus ten in half an hour. You'd look out and it would be clear. Next thing – *boof* – blizzard coming. Out of nowhere. It really isn't a nice place. The people are arseholes, they've still got pictures of Maggie Thatcher everywhere. It's dark, it's cold. There's nowhere to go. I was doing five weeks on, three weeks off. It took three days to get there, three to get back. That was classed as your leave. To my mind, it wasn't safe.

That's why I came off. If you can't do the job properly, you may as well not do it at all. I don't mind the strain on my body, I can deal with that. But it drained me mentally. I was depressed. I had to have ten weeks off after that job.'

'Did you see any penguins?'

A brief smile lifted the heavy trapezium of his face.

'Aye. Loads of them. There's something like five million on the island.'

'I'd be more scared to work on Piper B,' I said. 'It feels like an unlucky platform.'

He nodded soberly.

'You do get scared. When they bring the containers on board at night, and you hear them: *boom!* You're working on a floating bomb. A floating bomb that's just waiting for an ignition source.'

A platform, he said, was like a pressure cooker. There were quantities of oil and gas on board, a cache you could never forget, since the fumes hung over the platform, got sucked into the HVAC and pumped into the cabins, so you woke up with a sore head and a churning stomach. The calm, flat days were the worst, since there was no breeze to carry them away.

More than that, the human element felt explosive. A hundred men of varying temperaments, trapped together in a steel box, miles from land, from any sign of civilisation. The cabins were small. The bunks were narrow. The rec room was twenty foot by twenty foot. Your quality of life was contingent on everyone observing a few tiny courtesies: wipe your spit off the taps when you clean your teeth; mop your piss off the toilet seat; rinse your stubble away, don't leave it in a grimy ring around the sink; check with your cellmate whether they want the late or early shower, then give them an hour alone afterwards ('room rats' – men who commandeered the cabin all night, and refused to give their cell-mate even five minutes alone – were more reviled offshore than actual rats). Grievances that simmered over two weeks would come to a rolling boil, given three.

'It used to be a man's environment. If you had a problem with someone, you'd deal with it like a man. You'd sit down with them and go: "What's your problem?" Now, there are that many different nationalities on there, you can't have that face to face no more. Half the crew don't speak fucking English. I saw fights in the Falklands. Knuckles are rubbing now. People aren't happy about being replaced.'

'Replaced how?'

'If people are losing their jobs, where are all the rigs that have shut down? There are no rigs in docks. No rigs stacked up anywhere. They're still operating. They're replacing the people on them. I've seen it over the years. It started off that they replaced the cleaners. Then it went night shift, then they started going "We'll swap crane ops out". What's the point in paying you two hundred pounds a day, if they can pay a Romanian eighty pounds a day to do the same job?'

The man glowered down at the table as he talked, like a bulldog faced with a Rubik's cube. History's lessons were there for the taking. To ignore them was gross negligence. Piper Alpha followed the '86 downturn, when they got rid of good people, and kept the ones who cut corners and bent rules. Of course, they could no longer sack people arbitrarily. They had to create a paper trail, adhere to a slyly coded matrix, scoring workers on soft skills like *flexibility* and *attitude*. All the same, people who were exacting, who had standards, who might argue with management, were fired. Dissent was being exorcised. Talking back had become one of those quaint, outdated habits that only the old went in for, like taking your hat off as a funeral cortege passes by, or standing when a lady enters the room. Men with families to feed, and mortgages to pay, kept their mouths shut. NRB – the practice of blacklisting workers by labelling them 'Not Required Back' – was very real, though asset holders liked to pretend it was apocryphal.

'The S in safety is a dollar sign,' he said. 'It don't stand for nothing else. If they have to choose between losing millions and losing you, you know which one they'll choose. You're just a number to them.'

'Are you in a union?'

'Aye. Unite. I voted against three and three. Hardly anyone voted, apparently.'

A clattering came from outside. A wind was coming in off the water, whipping leaves and rubbish into little tornadoes, sending them whirling down the empty streets. Music was playing, very softly, behind the bar. The words were just audible, over the susurration of the game:

I know that you think it's fake
Maybe fake's what I like

I was suddenly hit by a wave of homesickness so acute I almost doubled over. Sometimes, I thought that was all Caden had been: an expression of severe homesickness. I rarely thought of home without thinking of him, or him without home, though he'd grown up more than a hundred miles away from me.

'People rarely act in their own best interests,' I said. 'I don't know why.'

'I saw this coming. People were getting paid fortunes for doing nowt. Cleaners on three hundred pounds a day. The oil industry has a short memory. During the boom years, they were paying silly money. Now, they have to pay all those people off.'

He was drinking very quickly. I noticed outside that he smoked with a similar intensity, cupping his hand around the ember and sucking ferociously, so the cigarette burnt down in seconds and developed a toppling mitre of ash. As I got up to go to the bar, he put a hand on my arm.

'I'll get these.'

'It's fine.'

'You're a lass. Can't let you pay for a drink.'

'It's tax deductible. This is work, for me.'

'You sure?'

Shower. His vowels had that same melismatic drift. Hearing it, I felt a tug of recognition in my chest. Old, pointless, vestigial love.

'Yes,' I said. 'I'm sure.'

When I sat down again, I saw he had taken his cap off. He looked older, less attractive without it. More striking, there was a large dent in his head. The central panel of his forehead had collapsed inwards, so in profile, it looked as if someone had taken a scoop out of his face. It didn't look like a boxing injury. It looked as if he'd been struck with a blunt instrument, repeatedly. A golf club, or a tyre iron.

'Other countries don't understand us,' he said, as I handed him his drink. 'We're chilled out, we have a laugh. When we take the piss, they take offence. And we speak so fast, we have such unique accents. Teesside is the worst for people not understanding you. The Americans don't have a fucking clue what I'm saying.'

'Whereabouts are you from, in Teesside?'

'Billingham. About five miles outside of Middlesbrough. A lot of the black trades come from the north-east. A lot of scaffolders come from Teesside. You'll walk into a building in Aberdeen and think "I know him from school, or from my local." It's probably why I ended up offshore. I had mates at school who always had the best of everything. Best trainers, best jeans. Because their dads worked in Shetland, or offshore.'

'What is it you do?'

'I'm a mech fitter by trade. I used to work at ICI. Then I moved into operations: getting the oil out the ground, cleaning it up.'

The bell rang for last orders.

'You're very easy to talk to,' he said.

'I'm trained to be.'

'I feel like I could tell you anything.'

I looked at him round-eyed, and tried to keep the sly note of journalistic enquiry out of my voice.

'You can. You can tell me anything at all.'

'You must get lonely,' he said. 'Up here by yourself.'

I nodded, as if the thought had just occurred to me.

'Sometimes.'

'A word of advice. Watch what you're doing. Lads get a bit … *overexcited* when they first get off. It's only a few, but they let the rest of us down.'

'I'm always careful.'

'You got a lad?'

'No.'

On the screen above us, a player was rolling around on the pitch, clutching his calf, his face contorted in agony. There was a stagey quality to the rolling, the agonised face pulling, that convinced me it was fake. Real pain is private, and largely inexpressible.

'Look at that,' I said. '*What* a performance.'

'Can't believe a pretty girl like you is single.'

'I'm not a girl.'

He gave me a long, proprietary look. I registered – then suppressed – the instinct to gather up my bag and get out of there.

'You look like one.'

'I'm thirty-four.'

'You don't look much older than my daughter.'

'Then your daughter,' I said carefully, 'must look old.'

I felt regret then, that I'd told the truth. Regret mingled with resentment. If there was a statute of limitations on defining yourself as the discarded mistress of a liar, I was fast approaching it, but increasingly I was getting myself snared in this type of conversation, and invoking the ownership of another man was the quickest way out.

'I did have a boyfriend. We broke up.'

'Not over it?'

'Not really.'

'Was he from here?'

'He was from Stockton.'

'I'll probably know him. What's his name?'

I smiled and shook my head.

'Still keeping his secrets?'

'Force of habit.'

His eyes roved my face. On the train, he'd appeared sharp, observant, but now there was a visible lag to his responses, as he processed my words through a glaze of alcohol.

'You good at keeping secrets?'

'Sometimes.'

He was holding his cap in both hands. His cheeks were flushed, though the room was cold enough that I'd kept my jacket zipped up. He gestured to my phone.

'That thing switched off?'

I turned it off and dropped it into my bag.

'It is now.'

'I killed someone. About ten year ago.'

'On purpose?'

'Aye.'

My eyes slid back to his scar. There were deep lines running across his forehead, so deep it looked as if the flesh had been etched with a Stanley knife. They veered diagonally across the concavity, before resuming their course on the other side.

'What happened?'

'I was tried for it. Acquitted. Lack of evidence.'

'No, I mean … why did you do it?'

'I had to.'

'But *why*?'

'Because I had to. People do what they have to do.'

His manner, supplicant a few moments ago, turned bored, almost dismissive. The celebrity batting away the gossip column- ist, grubbing around in the dirt for tittle-tattle. I looked around again. The two men at the bar had gone and the room was empty. It occurred to me that he might be making it up. It would be a strange lie to tell. Then again, it would be a strange truth to admit to. If he was prepared to tell me, a woman he'd met only hours before, then how many *other* people had he told? Maybe he was unburdening himself, as a person might to a priest. Except the ease with which this confession slipped out suggested he didn't find it very burdensome. So maybe he told everyone. Or maybe he saved it for women, the ones who looked like they were excited by the possibility of violence.

'You should keep that information to yourself,' I said. 'Unless you want to go to jail.'

As we stood up, I realised I was drunk. The man's big face kept sailing in and out of focus. He offered to walk me home. That way, he said, he wouldn't have to worry about me. I thought about saying no, but found myself stepping aside so he could lead the way out. What was the worst that could happen? The worst had already happened. And here I was, marooned on the other side of it.

We went up the stairs, making several wrong turns on the way, roaming the carpeted corridors of the hotel, going back and forth through the same heavily hinged fire door. When we stepped outside, the air was cool. There was an estuarine tang on the breeze. I trailed in his wake as we walked through town, using his bulk as a windbreak. Some teenagers were idling by a statue of Edward VII, their dog running loose off its lead. I stopped to pet it, and the man snapped at me to leave it alone. I left it alone, and ran a few steps to catch up with him.

When we reached my street, I paused at the corner. I'd never liked this district after dark. The dock road was lined with old warehouses, connected by dank ginnels and narrow archways, and at night, a quiet came over the streets, a silence so complete it was unnerving. I could remember one occasion when I'd been so spooked I altered my course. Shortly after I moved here, I was walking home when I saw a man waiting at the mouth of one of the entries. He kept his eyes on me as I approached, performing the lone woman's calculus in my head: *How far am I from my door? How fast can I run in these shoes?*

As I drew close, he took one step back, into the recess of the archway, so his face was concealed in shadow. Until then, I had been determined to walk past him, but there was something so deliberate, so measured, about this move, I knew no good could come of it. I turned on my heel and walked back to the station.

'This is me,' I said, stopping a few doors before my own.

The man turned towards me and reached out. For a long, lurid second, I thought he was going to grab me by the throat, but he only plucked at the collar of my windbreaker and rubbed at the Gore-Tex absently.

'This coat makes you look like a little burglar.'

I considered – then discarded – the idea of saying it takes a thief to catch a thief.

'Thank you for walking me home.'

'You lied to me about how long it would take. I'll have to get a taxi back.'

A few streets away, a car door slammed. A solitary gull skirled above us. In my pocket, I closed my fingers around my keys.

'You know that thing you asked me before?'

He looked down at me, a blank expression on his face. The smell of alcohol was coming off him in waves. *Steaming.* That was their word for it.

'His name was Tyler. Tyler Accord.'

I thought it was possible he'd forgotten the conversation, though it wasn't an hour old, that this would be a confession without context. But then he stooped down and put his face next to mine. His breath was hot and laboured, his voice loud in my ear.

'Want me to kill him for you?' he said.

It was two scaffolders, and it wasn't exactly a fight. The first lad
– let's call him Jim – was already working on the rig, and was a
well-liked, placid sort of guy. Let's call the other guy Tom. There
was bad blood between them from working together in the past.
Tom got put onto the rig a few trips ago, on the same rotation as
Jim. He heard Jim was on this rig so started slagging him off to
his workmates, saying he would get a hold of him and 'kick his
head in'. Words are words and actions are actions and this all
came to a head when Jim entered the locker room one morning as
Tom was, yet again, running his mouth off. Jim confronted Tom.
Tom went to hit Jim. Jim isn't the slowest of lads and before Tom
could hit him, he'd already hit Tom in the nose, causing it to
bleed out all over his T-shirt. That was it. Tom ended up with
two black eyes, and hid away from the other lads for a while.
When people asked him what had happened, he said he'd walked
into a handrail extension.

EIGHT

NINIAN CENTRAL

'So basically, you hang around bars all day getting on the drink, then go the strip clubs at night?'

'Pretty much,' I said.

'Fuck me. If Carlsberg did jobs, like.'

'It's not actually as fun as it sounds,' I said. 'See these?'

I tapped my left cheek. The two men looked, obediently. A ring of spots glowed through my make-up, their sheen and high colour a contrast to the rest of my complexion, which was dry and dingily pale.

'Poor nutrition. Result of a vampire lifestyle. When I get home, I'm going on a heavy detox. I won't drink for a month.'

'You won't manage that. Not with Christmas coming up.'

'Christmas is ages away,' I said. 'You think it's closer than it is, because you don't count the weeks you're offshore.'

It was the last week in October, the air thick with ghosts. A dense fog had settled over the city, every flight was grounded. The pubs full of restive men, waiting for the backlog to clear. I'd found these two sitting at the bar near the station's entrance. One was blond and thin, with a beaky face and a faintly bedraggled aspect. The other was small, dark and dense, with a smoothly shaved head covered in freckles, like a hen's egg.

In my teens, October was the month my best friend and I used to plan our 'new looks'. These plans were made to coincide with the academic year and the autumn/winter season, though they were less influenced by fashion than music. It was the era of the event video, the Hype Williams joint of broad ambition and limitless budget, when artists ran through five or six outfit changes in three minutes, and made sly cameos in each other's clips (weren't rappers *mates* any more, I sometimes wondered): Busta Rhymes, leading an elephant down the corridor of a sub-Saharan citadel; Janet Jackson, in silver contacts and severe fringe; Missy Elliott, bug-eyed and ludic in inflatable black; troupes of good-body girls in rain macs and Timbs. We used to take a pad of foolscap and brainstorm the new looks, writing notes like *loose, tonged waves* and *berry nails* and *green cropped fisherman's jumper* and *Dior hair mascara (red???)*. They had names like 'Rap Housewife' and 'Inuit Princess'. For two days, we dissected the looks, swore fealty to them, discussed character traits we might nurture to go with them. Then we forgot all about them until the next year.

Now, for the first time in my life, I was going into autumn with a new look, though as with many grown-up acquisitions, the process I'd gone through to get it was less fun than my teenage self might have imagined. I was thinner than I'd ever been, my metabolism seemed irrevocably bust, or permanently galvanised, depending on how you looked at it. Often, I forgot to eat at all. At night, I'd lie awake, feeling the mechanisms whirring, my mind as lively and chill as if I'd sniffed a line of flake. I stopped masturbating, and grew my pubic hair back (an exterior sign of an inward resolution, like a habit). I bought new perfume, an old-fashioned oriental, and wore more make-up. A full cladding of foundation, concealer, eyeshadow, kohl. Darker lipstick; a pink so deep it was almost plum. Three coats of waterproof mascara. Hollows of matte contour. I looked like a flight attendant, or one of those women who loiter by department store counters, spritzing bystanders with scent. I looked older.

One morning, a few weeks earlier, I had been woken by the intercom. I had no idea who it could be. No one in the city had my address. I looked out of the window. A white Range Rover was parked in front of the block, its engine still running. My mouth went dry; my heart started banging in my chest. I heard rapid footsteps on the stairs outside – the light tread of a little man – and opened the door with damp palms.

A maintenance man stood there. He said he'd been sent by the letting agent to do a spot check. Tears filled my eyes, and threatened to spill over. I asked to see his card, and he snapped that he already had keys to my flat and had knocked only as a courtesy. I told him, honestly, that he'd caught me at a bad time. I was still in my pyjamas, and barely awake. He called me a bitch, and left.

The incident had a chastening effect on me. That day, I packed away my fantasies and wrapped my mind around a few hard truths. He was never coming back. My mind had grasped this some time ago. My marrow knew it now. I'd planned my life around his rota so long, I was unable to stop myself calculating when he was onshore and off, but I stopped hoping, in the weeks he was home, that I would wake up to find a garbled text message, or a slurred voicemail on my phone. He was not going to appear on my doorstep, and admit that he too was miserable and had been waiting for my call. And though I saw him constantly (hanging around corners in the crepuscular gloom; standing outside the station, talking on his phone; hurrying down Union Street, shoulders hunched against the cold, or crossing the road just ahead of me, in pale profile), and felt an electric jolt of recognition every time, I knew it was unlikely I'd bump into him. He didn't live here. He only grazed the margins of the city on his way to work.

I knew I wouldn't meet anyone else and cheat my way to recovery. I went on a few dates, but it was like trying to treat a heroin addiction with Calpol. I'd come home afterwards and cry, so that my throat hurt and my head thumped, and I was ashamed to see my neighbours on the stairwell the next day. I accepted I was sick. I was sick, only he had the serum, and he wasn't going to give it to me, because he didn't think I deserved it. I had to do this alone. Without pain relief.

I worked, because that was all there was to do. I led a noirish half-life, getting up at twelve and going straight to the station, where I would take my first drink of the day. A better, braver person might have accosted these men sober, but I was shy and needed to drink. I struck a deal with the bouncer at the strip club near the station, that he would text me when the place filled up. I would come home from a day doing interviews and eat something, shower, change and go out again. I was tired all the time. My tolerance for alcohol soared. I switched from beer to whisky, telling myself it was the cleaner drink. It took an effort of will to unlearn my earliest training. I could see it on their faces, too: the tripartite psyche, tussling.

Most had been told not to talk to journalists, as children are adjured not to talk to strangers, but here was a woman, an *actual* woman, the first some had seen in three weeks, offering to buy them drinks in exchange for ten minutes of their time. I rarely took names. I never called myself a journalist. 'Writer' sounded more neutral, less liable to get them sacked. Group interviews rarely yielded much; there was a teasing quality to them, a depth-less back-and-forth. A disparity between time invested and divi-dends drawn. But every so often, a man told me everything. I'd catch him in the bar at the airport, or on the concourse of the station, and he'd give up all his secrets.

These men talked about home with an exile's longing, a perspective skewed by distance. The houses they missed were dolls' houses, the women and children inside arranged in tableaux. I was shocked, as I shouldn't have been, by the number that confessed to affairs, by the varied shades of connection that existed in the minds of married men. The many species that jostled for space, under the genus of 'extra'. Girlfriends. Side things. Shags. Sluts. Mistresses, of marriage-spoiling grade and potency. Ego-strokers. Attention donors. Other Women, in all their stripes.

At work, they spoke to them on disposable phones, or apps that left no trace. When they landed, they snapped the SIM cards, stashed the burners, wiped the apps. In a very real sense, these women only existed when they were offshore. At home, the portal slammed shut, and the girlfriends disappeared. Increasingly, I had to fight the compulsion to empathise, to jump in with the chummy anecdote, the time when *I* did this, and *I* did that, and not just because it was bad practice.

What I wanted, I realised, was my day in court, a chance to explain myself to a partial audience. It wasn't enough to tell *my* friends what Caden had done. I wanted to tell *his* friends, his colleagues, to shame him in front of his peers. My dream was of a chance meeting with people who knew him well, people on whose good opinion he relied. Then I could give my version of events, lure them over to my side with the clarity of my arguments. My favourite scenario – unlikely, but not impossible, given that the North Sea is a small place, and the weather was beginning to turn again – was that the cast of my first interview was somehow reassembled around the same table, minus him. I could fill them in on what had happened since that night, and together we would denounce him. Everybody would tell competing stories about his awfulness, and also comment on how well I looked; information they could pass on to him at a later date.

The temptation to say too much was always there. And there were times when, four bottles of beer to the good, my capacity for *voir dire* impaired, I did. Then, the man I was talking to might snap: 'Well, I hope you've learned your lesson now.'

More often, he tried to impress upon me a different kind of lesson. Sleeping with him would be a curative. I should ignore the signs and signifiers of his home life – wedding ring; trilling phone; rubicund toddlers and clouds of bridal white on his WhatsApp profile; once, memorably, a creased photo of a five-month scan, produced with shy pride only minutes before – and submit to his care. It only has to be once, he'd say. Just once. If we don't now, we won't be able to ever. And everyone's allowed one slip. I do everything for her, but she doesn't appreciate me. She hates it when I do anything for myself. She's jealous, she's controlling. She has no idea how hard I work.

By then, I'd picked up a smattering of the language, as an expat picks up a few phrases after six months in the new country. *My ex is crazy*: I treat women poorly. *My ex is controlling*: I am a cheat. *My ex is bitter*: I am incapable of linking cause and effect. *My ex took me for everything I had*: she received an amount commensurate with her contribution to our marriage. *My ex won't let me see the kids, though I pay through the nose*: I think maintenance payments ought to work like a VIP concert ticket, where you buy access to the performer, irrespective of my failings as a parent. *You're different to other birds*: I believe women are more or less interchangeable. I'd sit there, thinking that mothers who tell their girls they're special send them out into the world with a flank exposed. Occasionally, I asked these men why they got married in the first place. I got the same answer every time. *No man ever wants to get married. It's always for they girlfriends.*

'Who's going to talk more?' I said now, pushing my phone towards the dark man. For some reason, I was directing my questions to him. He had a sullen magnetism about him, the authority that comes with not trying. 'You, or him?'

'He'll have more to say than me,' the dark man said. 'He always does.'

I turned to the blond man. He began to talk, as if eager to live up to his friend's estimate. His rig, the Ninian Central, was notoriously hard to get off. (Whenever I said I wanted to talk to men who worked there, people made the same joke: *You won't find anyone, love. They're all stuck on.*) It was in the northern North Sea, and poorly designed. If the wind blew in a certain direction, hot air from the turbines' exhaust stacks flowed down across the helideck and into the engines of the S-92s, making them stall. But southerly winds were the least of their worries. Flights home could be cancelled for the stupidest of reasons: geese on the runway at Scatsta; ice on the runway at Scatsta (ice an apparently unforeseeable condition, in the Shetlands, in November); a pilot who couldn't fly in the dark; a missing bulb in the survival suit shed. Workers were sometimes still stuck there seven or eight days after their shifts finished, turning an enervating three and three into a dangerous four and two. Though most of the time, the man said, he got stranded going the *other* way. His life had always been like that. He was born lucky.

'I've got a mole on your rig,' I said, when he finished. 'He emails me his complaints. I heard there was a fight on there the other week.'

The men looked at each other. The dark man gave a startled bark of laughter.

'There was no fight,' he said, shaking his head.

'That's not what I heard. I heard someone got punched.'

'Did your mole tell you this?'

'I've heard it twice.'

This appeared to delight them. The blond man wriggled in his seat. He had a lovely, gurgling laugh, like a tickled baby.

'Were you in the fight?' I said. 'You *were*, weren't you?'

'Was I hell! Do I look like I could throw a punch?'

I had to concede, he did not. He was gawky as a Lowry drawing, all angles and elbows.

'Did you hear about it?'

'I heard the rumours. That's all they were. Vicious rumours.'

'*I* heard the rumours,' said the dark man. 'I heard it was more than a punch. A hell of a lot more than a punch.'

'What did you hear?'

'That's it. I've said too much already.'

'You two are no fun. You're rubbish interviewees, the pair of you.'

They looked at each other again and laughed. The blond man turned towards me, cupping his face in his palm, like a ditzy chat show host.

'I want to know who your mole is, me.'

I smiled complacently, and pulled my sleeves over my wrists.

'Journalists can't be compelled to reveal their sources.'

'*Haway.*' He dismissed my scruples with a wave of his hand. 'Tell us who it is. If I don't go offshore tomorrow, I'll forget all about this conversation.'

'A mole is an anonymous source.'

'Who does he work for? You must be able to tell us that.'

'I don't know,' I said. 'I don't know much about him, other than that he works on your rig and he's unhappy.'

'It's bound to be scaff,' muttered the dark man.

The conviction that scaffolders were lazy, stupid, dishonest, addled by steroid addiction, incompetent to the point of criminality, and given to telling pointless lies was shared by almost every offshore worker I'd spoken to.

'He says your OIM treats the rig like a fiefdom. And that his chopper always gets off on time. Whatever the weather.'

'I'll tell you something that happened last trip. I was lying in bed and heard two choppers come in – one was the OIM's flight – and they both managed to land, *smack bang* in the middle of the sector.'

'I heard he built himself a lovely new production suite that no one else wanted, even as he was laying people off.'

'Oh, I couldn't possibly comment on that.'

'What happened to the boy who inhaled H2S the other day?'

The blond man's elbow lost contact with the tabletop and his arm slipped off the edge. He righted himself and turned back to me.

'Now, how do *you* know about that?'

'My mole told me.'

'They're not even sure it was H2S.'

'What was it then?'

'Proper nosy, aren't you?'

'You have to be, in my line of work.'

'Aye. I suppose you do. Shy bairns get nae sweets, as they say.'

We gossiped idly as the light failed. They told me asset holders were trawling social media, looking for the aberrant comment, the errant opinion, that might turn a redundancy into a dismissal, a payoff into a freebie. Men were suspended and stripped of their positions, for being tagged in the wrong Facebook status. Some were moved onto the Murchison, which was little more than a slow-motion sacking, since the rig was due to be decommissioned in March. The blond man smiled when he talked about the Murchison. He'd spent seven years on there.

It was the happiest rig of all, because it was designed with people in mind.

They spoke about the conditions they worked in during winter, the horizontal snow and ninety-mile-per-hour gales that rocked the moorings and rattled the superstructure on its struts ('The rig is square, so when the wind hits seventy miles an hour, they er … well, they just tell us to *avoid* certain sides,' said the blond man, rubbing the bridge of his nose with a bony index finger). In December, it started getting dark at half two. The wind chill could drop to minus twenty. The platforms were so old, water swilled all over the decks. Yet still they were hustled out the tea shacks in all weathers. What they were witnessing was a systematic stripping of their rights, a kind of reverse Maslow, an inverted triangle of provision.

The blond man had been offshore more than a decade, and this was the lowest he'd ever seen morale. How could you feel happy when your pals were being paid off? He'd watched as friends missed holidays and funerals. He'd seen sick men stuck on the rig, when they should have been flown off.

Getting home on time was treated as a minor miracle, but any talk of transfers swiftly squashed. Lucky to have a job, they were told. There were men contacting their companies, offering to do their first trip for free. Offshore was overrun with a new breed of worker: the six-week wonder. Self-employed, armed with a quick enhancement course, they were taking jobs off real tradesmen, and charging more besides. Domestic plumbers turned pipe fitters. Welding inspectors who'd never held a set of welding tongs in their life. They were mercenaries, kitted out for the new era: high day rates, no rights. This was raw capitalism, free enterprise distilled down to its essence.

'I met someone who worked for your company last night,' I said. 'An ex-Marine. He was a sniper in Iraq. He told me he'd killed a lot of people.'

'He'll be a scaffolder, craic like that,' said the dark man. He kept crossing his arms high over his chest when he spoke. He was doing it now, tucking his hands into his armpits and frowning, like a disgruntled teddy bear. 'They're full of shit. Honestly.'

The blond man giggled.

'He'll be lying to you, you know.'

'He *wasn't*,' I persisted.

I was treating the story as a comic interlude, though at the time, I'd been nervous. As he sank treble whiskies, the man's lucid, funny answers had descended into paranoid rambling about government conspiracies and contract killings. Leaning against the slatted wooden walls of the pub, bearded and wild-eyed, he had reminded me of a shipwrecked sailor, driven mad by dehydration. This is what men always fail to grasp about women. We are scared of them, especially when they drink.

'He did seem a bit tapped. He tried to grab my head and kiss me in the middle of the pub. I ducked out of the way and he said: "This will be addressed later." It sounded vaguely rapey.'

'*Vaguely* rapey?' said the dark man.

'You didn't let him go to the bar for you, did you?' sighed the blond man.

'You didn't wake up with him, did you?' said the dark man.

'No. I didn't. And by the way, he was a plumber.'

'House mouse!' they yelled in unison.

A group of men burst through the doors, as if buffeted in by a gust of wind, and dumped their kit bags on the floor. The blond man went to the bar. I asked his friend where he worked. The Tiffany, he replied. My palms prickled.

'Don't think I know anyone on there,' I said.

Yeah you do. Caden appeared at the man's shoulder. I blinked to dispel the vision (it came in through the door with the wind; I could feel it). *Go away,* I said. *Stop interrupting. You're a nuisance.*

'Aye, well it's quite little,' the man said, with a modest tilt of his head. 'Only about seventy of us, all told.'

'That sounds … *nice,*' I said weakly. Caden was still hovering at his side, showing no inclination to move. I averted my eyes. 'Cosy.'

'It's a fucking shithole.'

'What do you do on there?'

A smile tugged at the corner of his mouth. He had dimples, two indentations so deep and perfectly round, they looked like they'd been depressed with a pencil.

'I'm a scaffolder,' he said.

The sky, just visible through the vaulted glass ceiling, was growing dark. The quality of light inside had changed, taking on a cool, greyish cast. A couple of corseted witches and an imp with a curling tail ran past the window and up the main staircase, their shrieks echoing across the empty concourse. The dark man levered himself off his stool. He had a train to catch. I fluttered four fingers in his direction. 'Watch what you're doing there,' called the blond man, to his back. I glanced at the clock on the wall. I was always rushing now, always aware of how much time I'd squandered, how little I had left.

'I should go,' I said. 'I've got my friend's leaving drinks.'

'Need a new friend?'

We looked at one another, the what-shall-we-do-now indecision of unsupervised children playing over our faces.

'I can't really be bothered.'

'Don't bother, then. Come the betting shop with me.'

'Will you be around later?'

'Might be,' he said.

★

Said was leaving. His company had laid off all its graduates. They weren't being seconded to Brunei. They weren't being seconded anywhere. He was moving home, to train as an accountant. The world, he said, would always need accountants. The back to back was off to France, to do a ski season. And after that, who knew?

I felt put out by their defection. It struck me as a waste of all that education to abandon oil completely. That was the difference between us. They were young and unsentimental. They knew about the sunk cost fallacy.

I should have tried harder with Said, I thought, as I walked across town. Except he belonged to those weeks in early summer, a time designated, with the binary process that attends a broken heart, as 'before'. Said was inextricably linked with 'before'. I saw him most days, and when we didn't see each other, our phones chirruped all day, with the chatter of new friends who can't stop finding things in common. I thought it might hurt, and pitch me backwards, to see him. Then again, I couldn't remember the last time I'd gone out for a drink and not pushed my phone under the nose of the person opposite.

I saw the back to back first. He was leaning gracefully against a balustrade at the edge of the annexe, talking to a blonde girl, with a bored look on his face. He held out his arms and greeted me as one of his own. I had crossed a physical frontier, and was like him now. Narrow, contained. A questing little switch of a person.

I was surprised again by the heat he gave off. He always looked to me as if his touch should be cold. I suppose I'd based this assumption on his white skin, his slippery, catlike style of attachment.

'Where the fuck have you been?'

'Mmm,' I said. 'You're all *warm*.'

He placed his hands on my shoulders and held me at arms' length. The blonde girl gave me a look that suggested she didn't much care where I'd been, she only wished I'd go back.

'I'm serious. Where have you been? I thought we were going to see loads of you.'

I bit down the impulse to apologise. I felt genuine regret, but as usual, my pity was self-directed. Things might have been better if we'd stayed friends.

'I don't know. I had my friendship butterfly net ready and everything. It's just ... nothing here worked out the way I planned.'

'Aye.' He looked around the room ruminatively. 'I know what you mean.'

'I'm sorry,' I said. 'Said told me. I meant to say.'

'Don't be. I hated my job.'

'You'll get something else.'

'Aye. I expect so.'

'No.' I put my hand on his arm. 'That came out like a platitude. I meant *you* will get something else. You're so bright. You could do anything. If I ran a company, I'd give you a job. In fact I'd *create* a role, just for you.'

'See, this is why I love it when you come out. My life is one long series of disappointments. And you manage to make me feel better about myself.'

'You *should* feel good about yourself,' I said. 'You're a gorgeous person.'

Said was watching us, an unreadable expression on his face. Whenever we talked, I got the feeling, difficult to rationalise but harder still to shake, that I'd upset him. We were cordial, but the air between us hummed with notes of grievance and concession. My invitation that night had the feel of a pardon, as when an errant duchess is restored to fashionable society after an internment on the fens. It's possible I was being paranoid, but this summer's events had transformed me. I ascribed to the creed of instinct now, and was sure, in the space behind my solar plexus, that I'd made him angry.

'How have you been?' he asked. His kiss felt cool against my cheek.

'I'm all right.' I realised with a shock that this was almost true. If not quite all right, then better than I'd been for some time. 'Busy.'

'Yeah? You look good tonight.'

He was appraising me carefully, the way you might a snake in a tank, or a large, untethered dog. *Can it get out? Will it bite?*

'Does that mean I normally look horrible?'

'You know that's not what it means. Why do women have to take everything the wrong way?'

We both fell quiet. I felt a powerful craving for a cigarette.

'It's my new look. I'm channelling Valeria out of *Narcos*.'

He pulled his mouth down at the corners and nodded.

'Well. It's working for you.'

'Said?'

'Yeah?'

'Fuck Deutag. Really, fuck them. Some people wouldn't know a good thing if it came up and slapped them in the face.'

'You're right,' he said. 'Fuck Deutag. And fuck Aberdeen. It's too fucking cold up here, anyway.'

A silence settled between us. I glanced over, towards the terrace.

'I'm going to go … *that* way. To the smokers' enclosure.'

'Hey.' He tugged me back, his fingers on my wrist.

'What?'

'Open your hand.'

'*What?*' I said, half smiling. I felt the instant resistance of the person told to shut their eyes, stand still, stay there. My hand remained by my side.

'Open your hand and you'll find out.'

I opened my hand. He eased a small plastic bag out of his hip pocket, and tapped at the edge of it. A few dun crystals fell onto my palm. I licked my hand, winced, and reached for his beer. That taste. I'd never get used to it.

'Thank you,' I said, swallowing.

He smiled at me wanly.

'Any time.'

Things come full circle. That circuit closes quickly in a small city. I stepped out into the wet air and lit a cigarette. This was where Caden and I had sat, the day he tried to make me wear heels and a dress. It was hot, June. The sun beat down on the annexe, the succulents released their damp breath, the leaves outside pressed in against the panes (as the night pressed in upon them now). The room felt like a giant terrarium, but with a slatted beech floor instead of soil. It was the same day we invented the messy-haired baby. *I invented her.* We used to say that at school, about timid girls we invited out, who grew into late-flowering social successes. *I invented her; she's my best invention. No, you didn't, I did.* I invented Said. Or maybe he invented me. What did it matter now? We were both leaving.

'She fucking *loves* you, doesn't she?'

The back to back had crept up behind me. The blonde girl was on the other side of the glass, talking to her friend. Her profile was tense and unhappy. Her eyes kept flicking towards the terrace. She saw me looking, and looked back. Her expression said she wanted me dead. That she hoped I'd die in an offshore fire.

'You don't have to sound so pleased about it. What's her problem, anyway?'

'Oh, nothing. We've fucked a few times, that's all. I'll likely as not stick my penis in her later.'

'Really?'

'I reckon. What's wrong with that?'

I shrugged with one shoulder and dropped my cigarette into a puddle. Water dripped, from the overhanging roof, the gutters, the bald trees bent confidingly over the deck.

'Stop canvassing for attention off other women, then. Go in and talk to her.'

Though I'd only just extinguished mine, I eyed his cigarette with envy. I was a person with too many vices. When I left Aberdeen, I'd cleanse myself of them all.

'You coming Tunnels?'

I shook my head.

'I'm meeting someone.'

'Hot date?'

'Hardly.'

'You're no really dressed for the weather. In your onesie.'

'It's a *jumpsuit*.'

He smiled. That heartbreaking set of slanted teeth.

'Same thing but.'

The haar was rolling in off the water, snaking up the streets in damp tendrils. The streetlights cast thin pools around them, but did little to penetrate the mist. Columns of moisture danced in the anaemic orange glow. I wrapped my arms around myself and hurried. I *was* inadequately dressed, as ever. Women from the north of England don't know how to dress for winter. That's how the joke goes. They'll wade through snowdrifts in no coat, naught but a 3.1 Phillip Lim playsuit and four layers of fake tan between them and the elements. The truth was, there was no way a woman could dress for the Aberdeen winter, not if she bought her clothes in Britain. Aberdonian winters were cold on a cruel, Scandinavian scale. It was cold from another era, a cold with no place in contemporary culture. Before I moved here, I thought I knew what it was to be cold, languishing in the Liverpool damp, or on a comparatively crisp day in London. On this, as on so many other matters, I'd been wrong.

The blond man was waiting for me in a bar off Bon-Accord Street. I divided Aberdeen bars into three categories: tacky, rough and boring (some occupied two camps at the same time, like the intersection on a Venn diagram). I tried to avoid this one, having designated it 'tacky and boring' some months ago, but like everywhere else that night, it was busy. People were spilling out of the doors and onto the courtyard in front, and the large, square bar in the centre of the room had long queues on either side. The staff floated around in their wooden corral, polishing glasses and wiping down surfaces with luxurious slowness. The man asked what I wanted to drink and I told him to surprise me. He did, bringing me a cocktail I couldn't identify, and would never have ordered for myself. It was dark, strong, overpoweringly sweet. A fat maraschino cherry bobbed among shards of ice, like a buoy stranded on an ice floe.

'They're offshore, aren't they?' I said, nodding towards a group on the other side of the bar. They were dressed in polo shirts and tight jeans, with sleeves that ran down over their hands, and random sections of hair shorn off. More than that, their young faces burned, with a votive, resolute Englishness.

'I think so,' said the man. 'Can you spot them dead easy now?'

I looked at them again.

'It gets a bit harder with men your age. But ... the young ones all look alike.'

'Bet you'll miss them when you go, won't you?'

The question surprised me. I'd never considered it before. Talking to the men was my job. A job I'd invented for myself, admittedly, but one that still came with the same tracts of boredom, the same sense of imposition, as a nine to five.

'I suppose so. They're the nearest thing I've got to colleagues.'

'I don't know how you've managed it, if I'm honest. If I'm stuck up here two days, I start getting dead bored, dead lonely. I hate being on my own.'

I skewered the bobbing cherry, and looked at the man again. In the half-light, his pupils were large, and his eyes were beginning to cross. His pale hair stuck up in tufts, like clumps of feathers. He looked as if he'd spent the night in a skip.

'What?' he said. 'What's funny?'

'Just you. Some things you can tell about a person straight away. It's so obvious you'd be like that. That's not an insult, by the way. It's to your credit, that you like other people.'

We were sitting in a booth at the edge of the dance floor. The music was loud, and we had to yell into each other's ears to make ourselves heard. There was a group of young women on the next table, with discreetly expensive bags, and long, glossy sheets of hair. One was wearing amber-coloured contact lenses with vertical slits of pupil. Another displayed long white incisors, bevelled into fangs when she laughed. Aberdeen Princesses. When men complained about them, they were really complaining about the city's character: close, money-minded, austere. These girls localised their discontent, gave it a name.

When I saw them, I felt loneliness of a different grade. I missed my friends, I thought, as I watched them move onto the dance floor. How carelessly I'd thrown them away when I moved here. It takes years to know a person, for those connections to bed down and mature, and I'd discarded mine, as if friendships of similar quality could be struck up in the space of six months.

'Let's go somewhere else,' I said. 'It's too noisy in here.'

'Monkey House?'

I shook my head. The Monkey House was another intersectional venue, filed under 'tacky and rough'.

'What about your hotel? We can have a drink at the bar.'

'It's full of knobheads.'

'Yeah. The kind of knobheads I'm trying to interview.'

'*No*,' he said, with unexpected firmness. 'I'll see enough of them over the next three weeks.'

I looked over at the group on the other side of the bar. Deracinated Englishmen. Boys, by any objective measure.

'You know, I did my first ever interview in your hotel. There was this horrible man there. *Jason*. He called me a whore. I stamped out the interview in a mood.'

He held my gaze. His eyes were that flat, ferrous shade always classed as 'blue', though close inspection showed there to be no blue in them.

'It's not Jason,' he said. 'It's Jayden.'

'What?'

'The lad you're talking about. He's called Jayden. I know him. I know this story.'

My palms prickled again. Beneath the table, I pressed my fingers into them. My heart, immune to such ministrations, smacked into my ribs. I felt a tingling sensation all over. The force field of my past life, encroaching on my present. When I looked up, I saw he was watching me closely, calibrating his next move.

'I'm going to say a name to you,' he said. 'Caden Doyle.'

The North Sea is a small place. The wonder was not that this was happening, but that I'd had to meet so many men before it did. Briefly, I considered lying, and saying I'd never heard of him, but I thought that was the kind of thing he'd do. Rachel breathed close to my ear, my constant companion these days. *One thing I do not do, is tell lies. He will have told you that.* Country syntax, hometown grammar. A strict regard for truth.

Once, we had loved each other, with the force to wreck a home. As the weeks and months slipped by since, that love had taken on the sliding, treacherous texture of a dream. At the time, it was all too real.

'I know Caden,' I said. 'Not that well.'

He smiled, his pleasure in my company refreshed now we'd found a point of contact.

'You know, as soon as you said that, I thought: I've heard this before. I heard it the day after it happened. I said to myself: "There can't be that many journalists up here, that many lasses, interviewing offshore workers."'

'There aren't. Just me. As far as I know.'

'Caden's fucking *mad*. I know him from by ours. He's on one all the time.'

And then I felt the fury every woman feels, on learning that the man who broke her still breathes. Why was Caden even alive? What purpose could he serve? And why was he still going out, having a nice time, when he ought to be sitting on the floor of a featureless garret, weeping over my old text messages? There was something impudent, something hard-necked about his vitality, his insistence on just *being*, exactly as he was before. He was thriving; I was altered at a cellular level. It wasn't fair. It wasn't *fair*. He had killed something in me. He ought to atone for it by killing himself.

'Is he?' I said. 'I wouldn't know.'

The man's eyes rested on my face, as if they'd found some degree of comfort there.

'Wouldn't you?' he said.

Caden swam up in front of me again. Waterproof coat. Two deep grooves around its mouth. *I love you*, it whispered. *Oh, go fuck yourself*, I replied.

'Last time I seen him, it was up here. He was steaming. No bar would let him in.'

'Toy fighting, were you?'

He looked at me sharply, his head on one side.

'What was that?'

'Nothing.'

'Don't sound like nothing.'

The apparition was still there. It smiled at me encouragingly, like a parent at a piano recital. *Haway, just tell the lad. Can't libel the dead.*

I shook my head to dismiss it.

'Nothing interesting. Shall we talk about something else?'

Chopper's Eve is like Christmas Eve. It's the best feeling. You hear the stories about Super Pumas, but if one was coming to pick you up, you wouldn't care if it was a Chinook. You can't be superstitious. You walk under that many ladders, all day, every day. But there was this one guy I saw on the Taqa Eider. He was a lead scaffolder and wore leather gloves. Every trip, on his last day, he'd walk out onto the plant, get his gloves, and chuck them into the North Sea. It was a ritual. It was him saying: I've fucking done my trip. I am out of here.

NINE

CLYDE

'Home *where?*'

I was looking at his mouth as he said this. His lips were thin, and turned up at the corners. It made him seem cheerful, even when his face was in repose, the same effect as a genuine, organic smile. I couldn't look at him without smiling back.

'Stockton,' I said.

★

On my last night in Aberdeen, I went out with Ryan, who was the nearest thing I had to a friend in the city, now Said had left. One night, a few weeks earlier, he'd appeared at the mouth of a ginnel on the dock road and started talking to me. He had a slight limp, the result of an old injury sustained on the Ninian South, when he'd slipped from a beam, swung widdershins on his working rope, and smashed into the leg of the rig. But he fell into step with me easily enough.

'What's your name?' he said.

'Pascale,' I replied.

'Like the unit?'

'With an e.'

'Where are you off to, Pascale with an e?'

By now, I was so used to talking to strangers, there seemed nothing dangerous, or even unusual, about this little man emerging from a tunnel and engaging me in conversation. Chief among Ryan's attractions were his pockets, which were always full of cocaine, sent up by post from Doncaster, and so potent a single line would leave me short of breath, my brain shrilling with accelerated insight. As I sat there that night, tapping heaps of powder onto my kitchen table and chopping them into lines, I thought I liked Ryan – he had a soft, artistic soul beneath his shambling exterior – but I preferred cocaine.

This was as it should be. After all, I hardly knew Ryan. Cocaine had been my mordant companion these twenty years. In some ways, it was the most successfully negotiated relationship of my adult life. It didn't make false promises. It was frank about its drawbacks. And when I chose to cool our association, as I occasionally did, it didn't stand outside my door politicking for my return, or call repeatedly from seven different numbers, or pester me with unsolicited texts. It respected my decision, and left me well alone.

At three, Ryan called a taxi and I abruptly unloaded Caden's possessions on him: some never-used electrical goods, still in their boxes; a pair of shorts; four Hugo Boss polo shirts. I'd despaired of finding a man small enough to fit them, but fate has a way of tying up loose ends, and Ryan not only worked in the same field, but shared my ex-lover's dainty proportions, which made me wonder if being tiny was a prerequisite of the job. It pleased me to see him loaded up with the emblems of my old love: impulse buys; casual clothing.

The taxi arrived and Ryan disappeared into the night, black hoodie pulled down over his face, box-fresh appliances cradled in his arms. I closed the door, knowing I'd never see him again. One more gliding connection uncoupled. One more half-friendship dissolved.

I woke a few hours later, and packed rapidly. It was surprisingly easy to leave the things I'd bought behind. The winter weight duvets, the bird-bellied mugs, the white towels. They had no history to tether them to me. A few things made it into my luggage: the wool throw, the dog-faced cushion, Said's overpriced tin opener. It glinted at the bottom of the case with the same steely insolence it had displayed in the dish rack. It always knew it would be saved. When I dropped the keys back with the letting agent, he greeted me coolly. He had nothing to sell this time, and it wasn't that long since I'd called to complain about his handyman.

I arrived at the airport too early to check in, and sat in the bar, surrounded by a low wall of suitcases. Men were walking through the empty hall, their shadows pale against the white-tiled floors. They drifted about in twos and threes, loaded down with bags and looking demoralised, like deportees from some failed state. One sat down next to me. His face had a vaguely Asiatic cast – broad cheekbones, tilted eyes – though his hair was dark red, cut into a pudding bowl shape, and his skin was very pink, as if he'd scrubbed at his face with a hot muslin cloth. He wore a khaki tracksuit zipped up around his chin, like a boxer in mufti.

'I'm looking for men like you,' I told him. 'I'm writing a book about offshore.'

'You a journalist or something?'

His accent was a bit like mine, but with a trilled 'r' that sounded Welsh, and a chewy, Cheshire burr.

'You'd be doing me a favour. I've got too many men from Boro. I need someone from the north-west. For balance.'

The skew in my interviews, he said, reflected the numbers offshore. There were too many from Teesside. They were like locusts. They colonised the Clyde and every other platform in the central North Sea. Their numbers multiplied every time his back was turned. Which wouldn't be so bad, except they were awful to work with. If they weren't complaining about the food – they refused to eat anything except chicken parmo or egg and chips – they were talking too loudly in the rec room, using up bandwidth fighting with their birds on FaceTime, swilling their revolting, albumen-textured protein shakes while appropriating all the best machines at the gym, or writing *BORO BOYS ON TOUR* on the bathroom stalls in marker pen, as if they were still at school. In short, they treated the rig like an outpost of Middlesbrough, and work as one long lads' jaunt away. This is what happens when a whole town is transposed somewhere else. They get to thinking they own the place.

'They *buy* their tickets,' he said. His face screwed up in mimicry. '"Ooooooh, I've done this and I've done that. We're qualified to do this, and we're qualified to do that. I've got this ticket, and I've got that ticket." It's a scam! They just get them off their mates. Change this name, change that name.'

I tried to compose my expression and essay an air of surprise, as if it were somehow shocking to me that a man from Teesside might reject good food and tell lies.

'I used to think it was a north-eastern thing, Geordies included. It isn't. It's a Teesside thing. They shout louder than everyone else. They think Boro is the centre of the world. They think if they're not on the rig, the rig will sink. Some of the shit they come out with ... "At home, we do this, and we do that. At home, we get this, and we get that." You want to say: Listen mate, you are *full* of shit.'

He jabbed a finger in my direction. I flinched, involuntarily.

'What do you do?' I said.

'I'm a plater.'

'How did you get your start?'

'My ex-wife's dad worked offshore. He told me to go.'

'You look too young to have an ex-wife.'

He laughed.

'Mate, I'm old. Twenty-nine next month. I creak when I sit down!'

'Did he help you?'

'Nah! He wouldn't help anyone do anything. He was a tight bastard then, and he's a tight bastard now. Hang on ...'

He glanced down at my phone.

'Am I allowed to swear?'

I wondered then, as I'd wondered before, where these men thought my authority flowed from. To whom were they appealing, when they asked if they were 'allowed' to swear?

'It's fine. You can swear. It's only my phone that will hear you.'

He told me some things about his hometown, three junctions down the motorway from mine, but uncharted territory as far as I was concerned. This town was where people in that rich county washed up when they fell on hard times. The bankrupt; the redundant; the divorced; the dispossessed. It was a cultureless backwater, a place of no fixed identity, nearer Liverpool than Manchester, though there were United fans there, dog legged from their city, as there were Muslims in the Balkans, dog legged from their faith's most sacred sites. The only jobs that paid properly were at the oil refinery, though they came at a price. The air quality was poor, the rate of respiratory illness high.

The place had nothing to recommend it, yet people rarely left. If they were lucky, they made it to the adjacent suburbs, but the town exerted a strange and fascinating pull, one they felt compelled to stay in range of. Its close, mean-minded nature was source and symptom of this stasis. There was no new blood, unless you counted a sizeable traveller community who had pitched up some years ago and decided to stay. Everyone knew everyone else, and talked about each other without stopping. Self-actualisation was suspect, success assumed to be contingent. Crabs in a barrel, he said, draining his pint and wiping his mouth with the back of his hand.

'Sounds shit,' I said.

'You *would* think that.' He grinned. 'You're posh.'

'I'm not posh,' I replied (my ceaseless, whining refrain these days). 'I've just got a posh name. My mum was a teacher. She thought my name would give me chances.'

'And how's that working out for you?'

Rain ticked at the window behind us. The leaves were off the trees, the city grey and renunciate in the cool winter light. The calendar was bare too, stripped of festivities until Christmas. Not that long ago, I'd treated Christmas as an advertisement for myself and my life in London. The weeks before were a time of frenetic preparation: a time to diet, bleach my teeth, thread my eyebrows and tint my lashes; to cut my hair and straighten it with a solution of chemicals, to paint gel on my toenails, to inject an emulsion of hyaluronic acid and my own blood into the hollows underneath my eyes. Then I'd rotate myself around the pubs I drank in as a teenager, back when I'd had to live with unbleached enamel and virgin orbital sockets, and feel smug about how far I'd come, the distance I'd put between myself and the teenage rube I once was.

But now my own hometown's gravitational force had proved irresistible. I was going back for the foreseeable future, and the gap between those selves was going to close. As it turned out, the temporal slip I experienced when I heard new, garagey house was just a premonition, because the intervening twenty years hadn't counted for anything at all. Maybe I'd look up my old boyfriend when I got back, and see if he could be persuaded to take me for another spin in his car. I could tell him that my attempt to leave was a failed experiment, that I'd been method acting the part of an adult all this time, but that was over now, and I was free to come back to him.

We could spend the rest of our lives lacing trainers correctly, cinching Berghaus coats at the waist, settling old scores with rivals on the cusp of middle age, and generally adhering to every severe dictum he laid down. He'd been out of jail for some time now. Unless, of course, he'd gone back in again. Which was possible – probable even – given that life is just a series of looping patterns and sequences that all but the healthiest among us are doomed to replicate, until death.

'It's working out fine, thanks,' I said.

*

We crossed the tarmac together. On the far side of the runway, a group of men in yellow survival suits trooped through the drizzle and formed a ragged line. From a distance, they looked like a crocodile of children, trailing through town to nursery, harnessed together in fluorescent tabards. Apparently, workers had the right to refuse a flight in a Super Puma. But who would avail themselves of such a right, in a climate like this? Our plane sat queued for so long, it began to feel as if we might never move. I looked out at the prematurely darkened sky and plotted for the worst. What if we couldn't take off? What if we were stuck here forever?

I said none of this, but thought the man might be pricked by some of the same secret fears, because once the plane taxied across the runway and heaved itself up, up through rain and banked black cloud, I asked what we should drink to. He tapped his tumbler against mine and said:

'To getting out this shit city in one piece.'

The cabin was half empty, which would have once been unusual for a Tuesday, and now was not. It was silent, apart from the hum of the engines and the receding clink of the drinks trolley. The man peeled off his jacket, revealing lean white forearms. He was unusual in that he had no visible tattoos. Unadorned male skin was starting to look odd to me; blanched and defenceless, like a woman's face without make-up. His hands were long and slender, his fingers scattered with pale freckles. His legs were long too. Even sprawled at an angle, so his feet stuck out into the aisle, he didn't look very comfortable.

'Quite tall, aren't you?' I said, taking a sip of my drink.

'Always have been.'

A fourth whisky in my hand, I could feel myself floating above the currents of the conversation, above the very notion of consequence itself.

'Never understood the fuss about tall men. Women talk about feeling *safe* with one. But statistically speaking, a woman is more likely to be killed by her partner than anyone else. If you're concerned about your safety, surely it makes more sense to pick someone tiny, someone you could fight off?'

'I'm not going to kill you. If that's what you're worried about.'

'I'm not,' I said. 'I'm just … talking.'

'So you like shortarses? That's a pity.'

'Actually, I'm off them at the moment. My ex was small.'

He smirked down at me.

'Beat you in a straightener, did he?'

'It's not funny.'

'I'm sorry. What happened?'

'He only liked new things.'

Asked this question at any other point, I would have given a different answer. My thinking moved through phases and fashions, as I fastened the blame on various people and events, until I settled on blaming myself, which at least gave me the illusion of control. It was my own fault, for falling out of favour, for creating a surplus made out of myself. Some women were like gold: consistently valued, consistently wanted. And some were like crude oil: miserably susceptible to market fluctuations. But Aberdeen was miles behind me now, and the distance was a clarifying sting. For the first time, I saw the whole picture, as a glimpse out of the window in better weather would have revealed the whole city: its stone suburbs, its chain of dark forests and sloping fields, its chill relation to the sea.

My hand moved up to fiddle with the cross around my neck. It was an outdated gesture. The necklace was no longer there. A few days earlier, as I sat drying my hair, it had got snarled around the dryer. I watched helplessly as the chain wound itself around the dryer's spinning barrel, and the silver loop tightened at my throat like a snare. I tugged at it, and only succeeded in pulling it tighter. After a period of futile scrabbling – which felt like minutes, but was surely only a few seconds – it snapped in two places. Martyred by a crucifix. A new twist on the old fear of choking alone.

'He was married. He left her, for a bit. We were fine, until she found out about me.'

'Did he have kids?'

I held up two fingers.

'Twin girls.'

The twins. Always referred to in duplicate. His screensaver was a picture of them, in matching football shirts, standing in front of a freshly creosoted fence. I used to avert my eyes whenever he took his phone out, so their faces were blurred, featureless ovals, like the *douens* of Trinidadian folklore, or my early, impressionistic renderings of him.

'How did she find you?'

'I don't know how she got my number. She sent a text, pretending to be him.'

'Simple but classic. *Love* it.'

The man looked amused. He'd heard this one before. All that money spent, all that energy expended, to ensure we never felt cheap. But cliché outstripped us in the end. I remembered standing on the concourse that day, waiting to meet him. The tannoy chimed, reciting a roll call of never-seen northern outposts, names that nevertheless felt familiar since I'd heard them so many times: Inverurie, Elgin, Forres, Nairn.

I watched passengers boarding the train and disloyally wished myself with them, pulling out of the station, leaving him and this mess of his own making far, far behind. I thought about saying sorry, then decided against it. I knew if I did, it would be a matter of record, held against me, as it is when a driver apologises at the scene of a crash. In the event of things, I needn't have worried. It was held against me anyway.

'After that, things went very wrong, very quickly. He went home to get his stuff. And he'd call, every day, with these … *dispatches.* One of her friends went for him in a bar. It took his mother and cousin to get her off. Then *she* saw him in town and went for him. She had to be restrained by bouncers.'

'Home where?'

The man was eyeing me with renewed suspicion.

'It's not relevant.'

'Home *where*?'

I was looking at his mouth as he said this. Seeing the *trompe-l'oeil* tilt of his lips, I felt a foolish, reciprocal smile tug at my own.

'Stockton,' I said.

'Where? Speak up, I can't hear you.'

'Stockton-on-Tees.'

He slapped his fold-down table in triumph.

'What did I tell you? Savages!'

'That's nothing. He told me he'd once seen her pull a woman she was feuding with *over a wall*.'

The man shook his head, and smiled into his drink.

'Mate, the birds up there do not muck about.'

'He used to call me his heroin, but she was the one who was habit-forming. He couldn't stop capitulating to her. He used to jump up and run out the room whenever she called. And she was never off the phone. I saw then that they could get divorced, but it wouldn't dissolve their marriage. They were obsessed with each other. I thought he was going to faint, when he found out she'd been to see a lawyer. It's so public, I suppose. And she was going to get a lot of money.'

'Marriage is a racket. I've got three kids. My maintenance payments are *astronomical*.'

I ignored this attempt to wrest the conversation back onto his turf. When had the locus of my sympathies shifted from the bill payer back to my own sex? Perhaps when I ran out of money, and so stopped paying bills.

'That's when it started. Just little things at first. So subtle they'd be indiscernible to anyone else. He'd take slightly longer to answer a text. He'd promise to call, then forget. If I mentioned it, he'd say I was imagining things. And I almost believed him. Except I could *feel* it. I had this gnawing in the pit of my stomach.

When we talked, it went. But it always came back after a few hours. Like hunger.'

The man plucked the lemon from his drink and started chewing on the rind.

'Gut instinct,' he said.

'He was drinking a lot. Spending money like water. He kept switching his phone off and disappearing. I was sick with anxiety. I couldn't sleep. I couldn't eat. I thought he was going to die, or go back to her, which amounted to the same thing, in my mind. I got sleeping pills from the doctor, but they didn't help. The fear just drilled down into my dreams.'

I could still recall those dreams. Not so much their content, but their claustrophobic feel. He'd appear in front of me, walking into an underground tunnel, or up on stage – Aberdeen airport having been reconfigured as a dark, musty room with the look of a school assembly hall – before vanishing in a puff of smoke, with the soft pop of an old-fashioned camera flash. I was not the kind of woman who fantasised about white weddings, but once or twice I was visited by that dream's dark inverse. Me standing alone at the back of a church, dressed all in black, a respectful distance from his real family. I could already hear the tentative first phone call, the unlucky relative chosen to give me the news. If they decided I merited a phone call, which they might not.

'I think I got hooked on the randomness of his responses. I used to wake up not knowing who I was going to get that day. The nice, sweet, consistent man who gave up everything to be with me? Or this new, cold, chaotic person who I didn't even recognise?

'Things I said or did would elicit a completely different reaction from one hour to the next. He'd promise to come and see me, then say he needed space. He'd change his mind three or four times in the course of one conversation. Arguing with him was impossible, because he couldn't tell the difference between what was right and what he wanted. Rather, his wanting something alchemised it, so it *became* the correct course of action. It felt as if I'd lost the ability to communicate with him, the way I'd lost my school French. Only this wasn't a gradual process. It happened overnight.'

'You should have binned him.'

'I did try. And every time I did, he'd beg for another chance. He did such an *abject* line in apologies. Women always think there's some sort of relation between how much a man will abase himself and how sorry he is. All it means is he's good at apologising. Probably because he's had lots of practice. After three weeks of this, he went back offshore. He had the DTs. He was shaking in the mornings, and very paranoid. He got it into his head that both his phones had been tapped. He said we could only talk on the office line. I lost my temper, then. I said: It's up to you if you want to live like this, but *I'm* not letting some woman I've never even met run my life. You. Have. *Left*. Fucking grow a pair, and tell her where to go.'

The man yawned and passed a hand over his face.

'Can I lean on you?'

I lifted the armrest, and he stretched out, so his head was in my lap. He had a sultry, sleep-darted look about him, like a blowsy fifties film star. His lashes were so thick and perfectly curved that had they been on a woman, I'd have assumed they were false. They were the lashes of a cow, or a showgirl.

'Like your freckles,' he said, looking up at me through half-closed eyes.

'They're fake.'

'What?'

'They're fake. I draw them on.'

'No *way*.'

'Honestly. Rub one off.'

He reached up, and rubbed at the central panel of my cheek.

'Fuck me. So they are. They look so real.'

'They should. I've been drawing them on every day since I was fifteen.'

'This is why men have trust issues.'

'It must be very hard.'

Unthinkingly, I was running a hand over his hair, fashioning a rough parting with my fingers.

'Go on,' he said, closing his eyes. 'I'm still listening.'

'I can't remember where I was up to.'

'He was back offshore.'

'Oh, yes. It was obvious he wanted to downgrade me back to mistress. But some processes can't be reversed. All this time, she was calling six, seven, eight times a day. The less he wanted to do with me, the more fixated she became on making contact. But he'd banned me from talking to her, so I never answered ...'

'Until you did.'

'I was writing about him. I needed a *dénouement*.'

'What was she like?'

I thought for a bit. How could I explain, how could I communicate, the long and spiralling horror of that night? Her snapping voice in my ear acquired a strange familiarity over those hours, her careless traducing of my character came to feel almost companionable by the end. I'd barely closed my eyes before she was calling again, with a long list of demands, the first of which was that I sign some sort of contract, confirming I was her husband's whore. I was going to be named as a co-respondent in their divorce, like it was 1922.

I answered the call with the bleary compliance of a sleep-starved detainee greeting a federal agent. Talking to her was a reminder I effaced myself too much. The world was full of people like this, whose entitlement dwarfed what they could offer. If I wanted to get anywhere, I'd have to stop loitering coyly at the back, and start shouldering my way to the front, alongside them.

'She was so great.'

'Was she?'

'No, of course she wasn't. She was twenty-nine and talked like a teenager. It was all *who was pretty, who was thin, who was clarty, who was a slag ...*'

'Was she good-looking, then?'

'Her pictures were so filtered, it was quite tricky to work out *what* she looked like.'

'I hate that. False advertising. I had one rule on Tinder: no filters. Any bird with dog ears or deer noses or flower crowns can get in the fucking bin.'

'Pity women can't do the same with men who filter their horrible personalities for the first six months.'

I kicked off my trainers, and tucked my feet underneath me.

'I told him so many times, "Whatever you do, *don't* say I'm just sex." I picked up the phone, and what was the first thing she said to me? *"He says you're just sex."'*

'Men always say that when they're caught.'

'If my husband left me, I'd rather it was for someone he loved than a hole between two legs.'

'You're different to other birds.'

I laughed, more derisively than I meant to.

'She kept saying: "It's just texts. He's left me for texts." In a way she was right. We'd only met six times. She told me some terrible things about him. She said he'd done this sort of thing all the way through their marriage. He was a fantasist. He lied about everything. He told lies when the truth was better. He falsified every single part of himself. Even the parts I thought couldn't be faked.'

'How's that?'

'Like … he used to get these erections that were so hard, they hurt. It turned out he was addicted to Viagra. Couldn't fuck without it, she said.'

The man stirred, and opened his eyes.

'He called the next day. He kept asking if I had any proof. I remembered something I'd read then, about liars. A person telling the truth will attack the assertion itself. Liars attack your lack of evidence.'

'Was he pissed off?'

'He was so angry he couldn't speak.'

'What happened then?'

'Nothing. Oh no, there was something, actually. Before he went, he told me I sounded *just like her*.'

'Heavy, that.'

'True story. He was a con man. Except he defrauded women of time rather than money.'

'You never heard from him again?'

The man looked sceptical. Clean break-ups were obviously going the way of candid photos and Brent Crude. In the beginning, I didn't believe it myself. I used to read our old messages every morning, and check his WhatsApp picture several times a day. It showed him in a field, wearing his mirrored sunglasses. I used to scrutinise it, trying to identify the tiny skewed figure in the lens, though I never could. Sometimes he'd appear online, and I'd almost drop the phone in my scramble to turn it off. Eventually, I wiped his number, and the cache of messages too. Seeing his presence flicker to life like this was too unnerving. He was lost to me, so completely he might as well be dead. Yet there he was, alive and well, in a separate dimension.

'Do you reckon he went back to her?'

'I don't know.'

'She would have told you. Birds are competitive.'

'You can't compete for a man unless he puts himself out to tender.'

'He had kids. That's a deal breaker, for a family man.'

'What makes you think he was a family man? It's so annoying, the way men always take each other's side.'

'Women do it too.'

'Oh no,' I said. I looked out of the window at the blank lozenge of night. 'No, they don't.'

'Which rig did you say he was on?'

'The Tiffany.'

'That's supposed to be a dump. All those CNR rigs are rotten to the core.'

'Then they suit him.'

'What was his name?'

I thought about refusing to say, then decided he didn't deserve my silence. I felt sure, if he ever found himself in my position, he wouldn't protect me with his.

'Caden Doyle.'

'Sounds made up.'

'Maybe it was.'

'So what now?'

It was a question so wide-ranging in its implications, I was unsure how to answer. What now? For the first time in my life, I had no idea. Our plans, which had seemed quite plausible at the time, now struck me as faintly punitive. A new baby. A cottage on the moors. A brace of redheaded stepchildren. An ex-wife whose mission was to never go away. Rachel really should have sat back and allowed us to trade futures, but poetry wasn't her strong suit.

'I always said I'd stop when I got to a hundred interviews.'

'What number was I?'

'One hundred and three.'

'What number was he?'

'One.'

He nodded to himself, an inner suspicion confirmed.

'I have to write them up, before anything else. Which will take weeks. I wish I had a slave to do all my transcribing. Maybe not a slave. An indentured servant.'

'What's this book going to be, then? A thriller?'

'More of a mystery. I wanted to see what men were like with no women around.'

'But *you* were around.'

'Yes, it was a bit flawed. Schrödinger's offshore worker.'

'Is it going to be dead racy? Like *Fifty Shades of Grey*?'

'I hope not. Have you read *Fifty Shades of Grey*?'

'My bird has.'

'Figures.'

'You got a name for it?'

'*Brief Interviews With Hideous Men*.'

'Bit harsh.'

'Sorry. Bad joke. That one's taken, anyway.'

★

The airport was deserted when we landed. The night outside lay black and impenetrable. At baggage reclaim, the man hauled me towards him, so my eyes were level with his chest. I studied his jacket. Close up, the fabric was crosshatched, the logo's crocodile rampant slightly raised. I resisted the urge to reach up and smooth it back down. The scent coming off him was familiar. Aftershave, fabric conditioner. The smell of a meticulously kept suburban semi.

'Like to see you again,' he said in a low voice, though there was no one around to overhear.

'I think that's a bad idea.'

Gently, I disentangled myself from his grip. He took my chin between his finger and thumb and tipped my face upwards. He was still smiling. He was unused, perhaps, to being turned down.

'You sure?'

Behind us, the suitcases churned. There was a thump, as one toppled over and fell onto its side. We both jumped.

'Maybe,' I said. 'I think so.'

*

My fears on the runway proved prescient, if a little premature. A few days after Christmas, a storm hit the east coast of Scotland. Flights out of Aberdeen were grounded, trains cancelled, roads closed. The Don, the Ythan and the Dee all burst their banks, one after the other, as if in synchronised display. Floodwater swept over the surrounding land, indifferent to markers of human permanence in its path. Sections of road crumbled, and fell into the water. The Dee rose up and up and up. Mobile homes were borne along its currents and tossed carelessly into bridges, like Pooh sticks. In the North Sea, with no mountains to protect its fields, the storm raged unabated. The Valhall field was evacuated after a barge broke its anchor and drifted towards the platform. So were the Eldfisk and the Embla. A man died in the Norwegian sector, another two were injured after a huge wave hit the COSL Innovator in the Troll Field. It was the wettest Scottish winter on record.

In the post-Christmas lull, the weather was the only news. Reports lingered over shots of collapsed bridges, burst rivers, sodden fields. People were shown punting to safety across lakes that were once main squares, canals that used to be side streets. My family kept remarking on my good fortune, as footage of ruined suburbs and soaked farmland spooled past. You got out in the nick of time, they said. Yes, I'd reply. I suppose I did. I was having trouble connecting the events unfolding on screen with my fate, though for a while, they were in touching distance. Already, I felt so divorced from the experience, it was as if I'd never been north of the border. *Après moi, le déluge.* Or something of that nature.

My money all gone, I found a job in a takeaway. By coincidence, it was in that last man's hometown. The town was made up of four big council estates, connected by a run-down high street. It felt like a backwater, a place cut off from mainland ways. It was like an overseas enclave of Spain, where no one ate their tea before nine at night. Several of our regulars worked offshore. They were contractors, oscillating between the rigs and the refinery, and they brought scraps of news back with them.

After the crisis, the price of Brent Crude picked up again, and companies began recruiting. Only this time, workers were being contracted to dismantle the platforms, plug the wells and ship the parts off piecemeal. The North Sea was shutting up shop. I thought there must be something uniquely depressing about this work; asset stripping, in the literal sense. Nothing to show for their efforts but absence, a square mile of sea returned to its natural state. Furthermore, these structures were the same that had kept their families housed, clothed and fed for years, and this work would be a continual reminder that their way of life was dying. If they had been cautious, or pessimistic, or both, they might have saved enough money to stay afloat while they worked out what to do next. But there would always be others who followed our government's improvident example, and imagined their luck would last forever.

I took an outsider's interest in the town, its grievances and blood feuds, its large, interconnected families and many-layered loyalties. Unemployment was high; a lot of people sold drugs for a living. Jail was a market risk, but it didn't necessarily affect the bottom line. If a person went to jail, his graft was passed onto his brothers, though as with any family business, it retained the founding partner's name. Customers lived in a permanent state of debt, strapping drugs from one outfit, then moving onto the next, until they exhausted all their options and had to pay back the first. Round and round they went, always owing nine out of ten.

The results of this shonky system of credit and remittance were everywhere. Often, young men – alumni of the same school of hard knocks my first boyfriend attended – came into the shop with black eyes, split lips, bruised knuckles. I learned it was part of the town's protocol not to ask questions, to pretend it was normal to walk around looking like this. Occasionally, I was called upon to break up fights at the front of the shop, and once, to order a boy to drop his girlfriend when I saw him trying to bundle her into the back of a car, as you might order a dog to drop a bone. I put the grille down and led her and her friend out though the kitchen. 'He won't change, you know,' I said, as I unbolted the back door. 'I keep telling her that,' her friend said. 'But fuck will she listen.'

Since my old job was a kind of licensed nosiness, it was perhaps unsurprising that the only part of my new job I enjoyed was standing around, gossiping with locals. All this stopped when our driver was sacked, and I was demoted to deliveries. He kept disappearing halfway through his shift with the money. He'd reappear the next day, always with a plausible excuse and the right amount, in the wrong denominations. Gambling, the owner thought. Or payday loans. Or both. The problems were co-morbid. So, like Annette Cosway, riding her horse in a tattered ball gown, I put on my old London clothes – my horse-leg boots; my leather leggings; my one good coat – to trudge up and down paths, delivering orders and accepting tips, until they were worn out, full of holes, fit for nothing.

I got to know the area quite well, better than many of the residents, whose loyalties tended to be tied to their estates. The town was going through a period of expansion, and there was a lot of development on the outskirts. Once, I was sent to a new address, behind a motorway junction. My phone made several attempts to find it, then gave up. As I drove up and down blind alleys, past empty warehouses and lumberyards, I became convinced the call was a trick, that I was about to be raped and thrown in the canal. Then suddenly, I rounded a corner and was on a gleaming tarmac close lined with tall, narrow houses. The houses didn't look like British houses, but were built in the Huguenot style, with gabled windows and Juliet balconies. Something about their spindly Cinderella proportions, and the plot's unlikely placement, made the whole encounter feel unreal. By the time I got back to the shop, I was starting to doubt I'd seen it at all. I tried to imagine living there, allowing my child to walk home through a deserted trading estate, or even attempting the walk myself, and could not.

There is usually a rationale to the way a town develops, a reason why people occupy one part and industry another, but these new estates defied all logic. They were just dumped on spits of brownfield and requisitioned marsh, areas with no amenities and few safe approaches. There were estates that overlooked the plant, estates that abutted the motorway, estates lapped by the foamy brown waters of the river, estates where the air seemed to fizz – a sound on the edge of sensation; a prickle in the atmosphere – because the lots backed onto the substation, or were hemmed in by rows of pylons.

There were large, flashing signs on the high street that monitored the levels of air pollution. *Bad*, the signs said some days.

And on other days: *Very bad.* Day and night, the refinery burned off noxious substances, which hung over town in a sulphurous cloud, adding a sickly yellow tincture to the sunset. At times, the shop smelled of rotten eggs, which I assumed was the drains, until the owner put me right. I came to understand the town's casual attitude to violence. What was a beating, a knife fight, as compared to this ceaseless environmental assault, the cost of chemical living?

When I worked in magazines, proximity to other people's money gave me an unearned sheen. Now the same process was happening in reverse. Increasingly, I resembled the customers. My skin lost tone. My hair began to break off and fall out. Photos from that time show me looking like a medieval pinup; pale, drawn, my forehead half an inch higher than it used to be.

A new boy replaced me on the counter. He was large and ungainly, with shrewd little eyes like bits of blue glass. He had a habit of standing in exactly the wrong place at exactly the wrong time. He could make a mess of any task: the physical world was mobilised against him. Once, he tried to put the vacuum cleaner away and got wrapped up in the wires, like Laocoön. The flex and the hose got snarled around him, and then around each other, and he spent a full ten minutes, turning this way and that, trying to fight his way out. People thought he was stupid, but he was actually quite clever. It was *part* of his cleverness to pretend to be stupid, to act the buffoon, so he could get away with doing nothing. I realised this when he told me he was taking A-Levels at college, and was predicted two As and a B.

'That's what I got,' I said. 'You never know. If you get your head down and *really* apply yourself, in twenty years' time you could be working in a chicken shop.'

This was a joke, but when I looked up, no one was laughing. The boy cleared his throat.

'How's your book going?' he said.

I was still going to the library every day, still writing, though the project had taken on the air of an alibi, a cover story I'd concocted to conceal my true vocation.

'It's going,' I said.

'What's it about, again?' he asked, furrowing his brow. 'Cranes?'

In quiet moments, we sat at the counter, watching people walk past. There were two girls I became fascinated with, who lived in the building opposite. They looked as if they might be related, except one was painfully thin and the other quite fat. The fat one had short hair she dyed a different colour every week: pewter, pink, green, like a parakeet's wing. I christened them (to myself) the modern tramps, because they did a lot of hanging about, in drooping clothes, like something out of a Beckett play. They were always getting locked out of their building. Every other day, I'd see one of them standing outside the front door, while the other stood behind it, rattling crossly at the catch. There was a slightly schematic quality to these incidents, a hapless choreography; it was like watching a silent movie, where the action centres around the hero dropping a bushel of papers in a high wind, or getting a shoelace stuck in a grate. Realistically, I suppose they only had one key between them and the lock was tricky, but distance, and my ignorance of their actual circumstances, infused their travails with drama.

'The birds here are so rough,' the boy observed. 'Why is that?'

'Because they're poor,' I said. 'Their lives are hard.'

'Do you reckon the pretty ones bag rich men and get out?'

I shook my head.

'It doesn't work like that.'

I gave him a lift home most nights. He lived halfway between the shop and my house, and I didn't like the idea of him making his own way back. I suspected him of being unable to handle himself, despite his size. He seemed ill-equipped to negotiate the town, its sly, volatile inhabitants and intermittent explosions of affray. 'Come on, Buggerlugs,' I'd say, jingling my keys. 'Let's get out of here.' *Buggerlugs*. A childhood name, one my father gave me, back when he could talk.

Driving down the high street, we sometimes passed people he knew. On these sightings, he'd offer muttered commentary:

'He went to my school. Absolute punny.'

And once, more approvingly:

'Shane Walsh. I follow him on Insta. *So* sick.'

I glanced at the youth in question as we pulled up at the lights. He was tall and well built. His face was round, without being fat, and his hair, in the murky fluorescence of the strip lights, could pass for red. When I first started at the shop, I thought of him often, and wondered if I'd see him again. As time went on, the possibility felt more and more remote. I began to feel as if I'd made him, and all the others, up. When I told people I used to live in Aberdeen, that I went there to write a book, it sounded like a lie, even to me. I looked again. It wasn't him: too young. The car behind me beeped. The lights had turned green.

At the refinery, the flare blazed high and white. Plumes of smoke rose from the plant, and hung over the river in thick banks.

'Is that on fire?' the boy said.

'They burn the gas off sometimes. It's meant to be controlled.'

'Doesn't look it,' he said gloomily.

I accelerated up the slip road. This junction was unusual, in that you approached the motorway from below rather than above, so you couldn't see the traffic until the very last moment. Many times, I'd winced and fought the mad compulsion to close my eyes as I pulled into the slow lane. The contingency of motorway driving, its scanty margin for error, still scared me. Part of me secretly believed the death I'd cheated twenty years before was coming back to claim me, that it had retreated to its corner but was only biding its time. At night, I'd lie in bed and see all my near misses and narrow escapes, every chancy decision and disregarded risk spread out before me in a wintry flush. Visions danced inside my eyelids and kept me from sleeping.

When I go to bed at night, I think of you with all my might.

Remember? Relate.

What might have happened, had I mistimed my attempts to merge with the traffic, if the lorry in the next lane had failed to see me, or refused to move over? If conditions were less favourable, and I'd gone slithering across the wet road and collided with its wheels, or missed it by inches, only to go slamming into the central reservation beyond? *What if? What if?* It seemed statistically impossible, in a world with so many avenues for grief, that I might glide by unscathed.

'Can I put my tunes on?' the boy said.

'Nope.'

'Why you got to do me so dirty all the time?'

'When you learn to drive, you can play whatever you like.'

'I don't need to learn to drive. I have you to drive me about.'

'You *do* need to,' I said severely. 'Girls won't like you if you can't drive.'

This was a shot in the dark. I had no idea what teenage girls did and didn't like. Certainly, it had been true in my day, but a lot of what the boy told me suggested that the established order of suburban life had been upended since then.

'Anyway,' I added, as an afterthought. 'I won't be here forever.'

The boy didn't respond. Unlike an adult, he never felt any obligation to make conversation on these journeys. He appeared unaware of the social compact that demands you at least reply to the driver once you've accepted a lift. At times, I'd catch sight of his bulk in the passenger seat and feel as if I had acquired a giant

teenage child. He was fractious when he first got in the car –
messing about with the seat, shouting into his phone, politicking
to vape with the window down, or play his music, just for a bit –
but once I'd refused him everything, he'd simply lapse into silence
and sit there, absently scrolling.

I moved into the right lane to overtake a tanker. This stretch of
motorway ran between the refinery and the oil terminal, and was
always busy, even at night. Articulated lorries drove in concert,
switching lanes as if they were nimble little hatchbacks. A road
ran parallel to the motorway, half-concealed by hedgerow. At
times, headlights would loom up through the greenery, giving the
impression there was a car on the wrong side of the road, heading
straight into the oncoming traffic. On the southbound side, the
land sheared away to the estuary. This was liminal, borderless
country, its boundaries shifting with the tide. Oily creeks made
causeways of the scrub. Ditches filled with brackish water and
spilled over the surrounding fields. On that side, the machines
claimed dominion. There were no houses, no signs of human life,
only factories and holding tanks, pipelines and distillation drums.
They said a boy died there, years ago. He fell into a vat of toluene
and drowned. That was an old story, though. No one remembered it now.

'Do people still drive to clubs?'

'Hmm?'

The boy looked up dazedly, as if I'd shaken him awake.

'Do people still drive to clubs in other cities? Then drive back
afterwards?'

'Nah. They just save up, go the fezzies.'

So that was that. A slice of English life scrubbed out. He would
never know what it was, to go flying through the night, a whole
subculture pouring from the speakers. MC Det in the mix, yelling
coded jargon, foxing the grownups: *This one goes out to the cotch*

crew, the bedroom massive. This one's all the driving massive, making their way to a rave. Time to close your eyes and reminisce (not if you're driving, though!). This one's Marissa, Kazia. And Mum: up north somewhere.

England was ours, inside those empty hours. We moved in convoy, commandeering the roads, the nation's arterial networks, as if enacting martial law. I thought of myself at sixteen: I didn't even register risk. The world was safer now, but so closely monitored. And something is always lost when human freedom is curtailed.

We sped west, through the sluggish summer dark. Ahead of us, the motorway lay flat and featureless. As I flicked my high beams on, the boy gave a strangled shout, and dropped his phone into the footwell.

'The exit!' He gestured frantically. 'You're going to miss the exit!'

Seized by panic, I slammed my foot against the accelerator. The little car surged forward, pulling ahead of a van in the next lane. Abruptly, I turned the wheel and lurched across its path. Unheeding of the horn's blare behind us, I kept my foot on the floor, sailed across the left lane and down the slip road. For a second, the car veered out of control, its tyres barely skimming the asphalt. I hit the brakes and we skidded to a halt with a screech and a patter, as an arc of loose stones hit the chassis. My heart was banging in my chest. My palms slid along the wheel.

'Sorry,' I said. 'I'm so sorry. I don't know why I did that.'

Beside me, the boy was shaking with laughter.

'You're heavy, you. Nearly took us out.'

I drove the rest of the way in chastened silence. As he got out the car, I said:

'You're not going tell your mum, are you?'

'Nah,' he said good-naturedly. 'I'm no grass.'

Dropping him off took me out of my way. I either had to turn around and get back onto the motorway, or cut across country, down a series of narrow lanes. The motorway was more direct, but I disliked the sensation of going back on myself, so I set off down the lanes. The route was twisting and tortuous; it felt almost counterintuitive. For most of the way, it seemed to be leading nowhere. At one point, the road went over a stream and up a steep incline, before crossing the motorway itself. As I drove across the bridge, I looked down at the other cars, manned by more hardheaded drivers.

On the other side, the road was very dark, and it took me a while to realise I'd made a wrong turn. Sleepily, I drove through tunnels of trees and into troughs of deep shadow, trying to work out where I was.

Summer had come on all at once that year, and the foliage was so thick and lush, the way ahead was partially obscured. But the sky was clear, the ordinance of the stars so bright, it was hard to feel completely lost. Eventually I emerged, as if from a trance, onto a road I thought I recognised. I'd never approached it from this direction before, but as I swung out of the junction, I felt quite sure. I was only a few miles from home.

ACKNOWLEDGEMENTS

To my family, for pretty much everything. To my early readers Eva, Tim, Lucille, Helen, Marissa and Sophy, for their encouragement and thoughtful feedback. To my longest serving friend Sarah Ellis, for introducing me to Jon McGregor. To Jon, for being so generous with his advice and his contacts. To Tracy Bohan, for believing in my book when I didn't, and for being the best agent I could wish for. To Jake Molloy and Sue Jane Taylor, for their time and their insight. To Catherine Twomey and her family, for showing me love in a cold climate. Most of all, to the 103 men who shared their stories with me. You didn't have to, but you did. Thank you. Thank you.